WARRIOR
PHARAOHS

P.H.NEWBY

WARRIOR PHARAOHS

THE RISE AND FALL OF THE EGYPTIAN EMPIRE

Faber and Faber
London & Boston

To Sarah and Katie

First published in 1980 by
Faber and Faber Ltd
3 Queen Square, London WC1N 3AU

Edited, designed, and produced by Guild Publishing,
the Original Publications Department of
Book Club Associates

British Library Cataloguing in Publication Data

Newby, Percy Howard, *b. 1918*
Warrior pharaohs.
1. Egypt – History – To 640
I. Title
932   DT83

ISBN 0-571-11641-8

DESIGNED BY CRAIG DODD

Set in Monophoto Imprint
and printed by W. S. Cowell Ltd, Butter Market, Ipswich, Suffolk

CONTENTS

1
THE CHALLENGE
OUT OF ASIA

BY EGYPTIAN STANDARDS AMON WAS
not a particularly ancient god. He was an infant compared with the falcon-headed sky-god Horus, the sun-god Re in his various manifestations, Osiris the nature-god who was murdered and rose from the dead, Set his brother who committed the crime, and Ptah the creator-god, all of whom emerged in remote times. He was not in evidence when the two countries of Upper and Lower Egypt were first united under one ruler in 3100 BC or thereabouts and he was still inconspicuous when the pyramids were built hundreds of years later. Even the city with which he is most associated, Thebes, was of secondary importance until quite late in Egyptian history, by which time the Great Sphinx itself was so old and neglected it was half covered by sand blown in from the desert by the regular storms of early summer. Thebes was the great city of the New Kingdom and Amon, its god, became the promoter of an unprecedented aggressive nationalism. This was in the sixteenth century BC.

His name means 'he who is hidden'. The doors of his shrine were never opened except by the king himself or the most senior priests. They alone could see him face to face. He was in human form but dark blue as befitted the superhuman. Like a king he wore a ceremonial beard but unlike a king's this beard was plaited and turned up at the end. He wore a short kilt with an animal's tail behind and a tall hat with two ostrich feathers. In one hand he held the sign of life, the *ankh*, and in the other a wooden sceptre topped with the carved head of an animal and with two prongs at the other end, an object which looks like the ceremonial stick of some tribal chieftain with his wealth in cattle and sheep. This is the *uas* sceptre, the symbol of power and dominion. But Amon was god of wind and air. As time had gone by he had annexed the qualities of other gods, notably the ithyphallic Min, to become a god of procreation. Most important of all, he assumed in his great ambition the status of the sun-god Re himself and wore a solar disc between his ostrich feathers to show his ultimate apotheosis. His sacred animal was the horned ram. Sometimes it was a goose.

Although he was made of gold-plated wood, had obsidian eyes, and was only a few feet tall, he was, so far as the king and the priests were concerned,

Previous page : The great hypostyle hall of the temple of Amon at Karnak is the expression in stone of Egyptian imperialism. It was completed in the thirteenth century BC by Ramesses II

Incense is offered to Amon-re as part of the daily ritual. On the wall of his great temple at Abydos (above) Seti I is using the traditional arm-shaped censer (below)

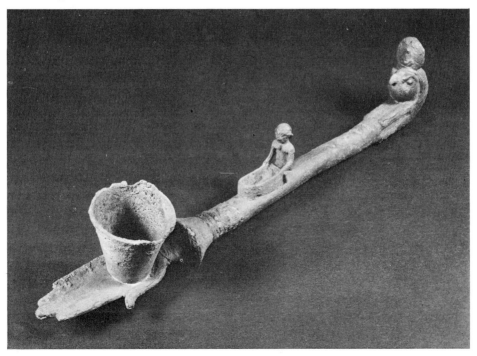

animate. The image was not the god himself – Amon-Re was not an idol – but in the presence of the image direct communication with the god was possible. In the Theban studio where he was fashioned, ceremonies were performed by the priests to ensure that Amon was no mere object of wood, metal, and precious stones. He was purified with water and natron, and fumigated with incense. An ox, a goat, and a goose were slaughtered. The foreleg and heart of the ox, together with the adzes, the chisels, and the other tools used in the making of the statue, were presented at his mouth. Hymns were sung, Osiris invoked – all to 'open the mouth' of the statue so that the god could fitly dwell there and function in the way expected of him: as an oracle, a decider between two verdicts or courses of action by giving a 'great nod', as an authority for all appointments to high office, even that of the king himself, and to be the supreme officiator at the coronation.

His granite shrine in the innermost, darkest, and most holy chamber of the temple had two wooden doors which were opened soon after sunrise every morning by the king or his surrogate priest. His toilet consisted of a change of clothing, fumigation with incense from a burner shaped like a human arm, a sprinkling with water, a cleansing of the mouth with balls of natron, a painting of the eyelids black and green, and other such attentions as befitted his status as a god, a king, and sentient being. An offering of honey was made. Other food and drink were placed before him; all this in the obscurity of a windowless sanctuary lit only by vegetable oil lamps whose smoky and wavering flames brought flickering mobility to the golden body and alert intelligence to the translucent eyes.

On a stone pedestal in front of the shrine was a ceremonial boat. On special occasions the god would enter the midship cabin and be carried out of the sanctuary on the shoulders of bearer-priests. These hairless and purified men in close-fitting white linen gowns intoned sacred formulae as they walked. In the great columned hall of the temple Amon-Re might exceptionally witness in acknowledgement of his divine favours the king clubbing to death enemy prisoners. Usually this was a symbolic gesture. In addition to the ceremonial boat the god had a Nile barque made of Lebanese cedar, sheathed to the water-line in gold, on which he was towed upstream once a year, on the great Feast of Opet, to cohabit with his queen, Mut, in the 'harem of the south' at Luxor. Once a year, too, Amon-Re visited the funerary temples on the west bank of the Nile to 'pour water' – make ceremonial libations, that is to say – for all the kings of Upper and Lower Egypt who were now dead and at one with Osiris but who had established foundations so that their memory might be kept green.

Opposite : Amon-Re represented in traditional style. This small silver and gold figure may have been used in a portable shrine
Overleaf : A late representation of priests carrying the barque of Amon-re

Amon-Re was not a bloodthirsty god in spite of the occasional human sacrifice because the Egyptians, by the standards of their time, were a humane people; but he was the god under whose guidance the pharaohs 'extended the frontiers of Egypt' – to quote the inscriptions – southwards into Nubia and the Sudan, east and north into Asia as far as the Euphrates. In his name Egypt came to dominate the civilized world. From time to time, then, pharaohs symbolically clubbed foreign prisoners to death in his presence – Nubians, Libyans, Canaanites, Hurrians, Hittites, men of Mitanni, the land beyond the Euphrates, Amorites, and even pirates from the other side of the Mediterranean, the 'Great Green' as the Egyptians called it. Egyptian gratitude for his many interventions was effusive beyond all modern reasoning; and it brought Egypt too, in the course of time, to its own special humiliation.

Egypt is a peculiar country, though no doubt the Egyptians would not have put it that way. Egypt, they would have said, was the norm and other countries were exceptional. When Herodotus of Halicarnassus went to Egypt about two and a half millenia ago, he said the Egyptians did everything by contraries, from cloacal habits to the rigging of sea-going boats. One, perhaps trivial, illustration of the difference between the way the Egyptians see the world and the way the rest of us do is provided by the simple question of orientation. Or should it be australation? The Nile flows from south to north. Upper Egypt is therefore the southern part of the country and Lower Egypt, including the Delta, is the northern part. The words 'north' and 'south' do not seem to have quite the same significance as in other parts of the world and the unwary traveller can easily find himself thinking that Alexandria, say, is some kind of deep south and that Aswan and the new High Dam are in northern territory, since they are upstream. It so happens that the ancient Egyptians took their bearings by facing up-Nile. We know this because the words for 'right hand' and 'west' were the same; so were 'left hand' and 'east'.

As the Nile for all practical purposes was the only source of water in Egypt, it was natural to refer to less fortunate lands which depended on rainfall as having 'a Nile in the sky' – and the king of Egypt, incidentally, was believed to have control of it, even in Asia. These foreign lands were, from the Egyptian point of view, labouring under the most enormous disadvantages. The Egyptians had been so long in their valley, continuously developing traditions and customs, that there was no doubt in their own minds that what went on in Egypt was in keeping with the divine ordering of the universe, whereas what happened outside their borders was aberrant and probably sacrilegious. Out there, in Asia, in Libya, and in Nubia the men and women were not, as Egyptians were, real persons.

The Nile between Luxor and Aswan showing the sharp contrast between the desert and cultivated land

By the time Ramesses II – or Ramesses the Great, as he came to be called – was crowned by Amon-Re just before 1300 BC, this Egyptian assumption of superiority over other people had been shaken by foreign invasion, immigration, and, paradoxically, the achievements of Egyptian imperialism itself; by it Egyptians were brought into contact with the ancient cultures of Mesopotamia, Syria, and the territory that had still to acquire its name of Palestine. But if Egyptians could no longer regard their neighbours as non-persons, they nevertheless thought it right and proper to aggrandize themselves as much as possible at the Asians' expense. Egyptian monarchs developed opulent tastes and a style of conspicuous consumption which ambassadors from lesser countries were expected to marvel at. Megalomania was almost forced on the pharaoh because he saw himself competing not only with foreign kings but with his predecessors in Egypt who, from the pyramids onwards, had left such striking monuments. Bigger and better temples had to be built, statues carved that were even more colossal, and obelisks reared that approached even nearer the daily voyage across the sky of the sun-god himself. If there was no time, or the resources were lacking, to out-do the dead, the pharaoh did not hesitate to usurp their monuments by substituting his own name for theirs. Great temples were plundered for their stone so that even greater temples could be built by the ruling monarch, usually with inferior taste and craftsmanship.

No pharaoh was busier in this way than Ramesses the Great. His huge temples and colossal statues are to be found, in varying stages of ruin, throughout the land of Egypt and beyond. No doubt he would have taken particular pleasure in the great cost and engineering skill required between 1964 and 1969 to rescue his Abu Simbel cave temples from the rising waters of Lake Nasser following the construction of the New Dam; these temples, with all their statues, were sliced out of the living rock and moved sideways and upwards to a new, artificial cliff. It is around the name of Ramesses that the cobwebs of regret for the departed glories of Egypt are usually seen to gather. A man who, in his monuments, set out as blatantly as he did to defy time and mortality is a sure candidate for the special obloquy of historians that emphasizes how unaware he must have been of the real forces at work in his society, that Egypt for all his gesturing was in fact dying and he ought to have been doing something about it. They are not necessarily right about his lack of perception.

Gibbon was sitting among the ruins of the Capitol when the idea first came to him of writing *The Decline and Fall of the Roman Empire*. Since time and chance happen to all, since institutions have youth, maturity, and falling off, like the men who created them, it is no great mystery why empires decline; what needs explaining is how they came into existence in the first place. If any prompting is required for an account of the rise and fall of the Egyptian empire – and it happened at a time almost as remote from the Romans as the Romans are from us – it would probably be found not at Abu Simbel or the great hypostyle hall of Amon-Re's temple at Karnak, for which Ramesses II was largely responsible, but in his mortuary temple, the Ramesseum in western Thebes. Inevitably it would be Ramesses who sets the mind working. The Ramesseum is a ruin. Here lies the shattered colossus that remotely inspired Shelley's sonnet, 'Ozymandias' – which, as User-ma-Re, was the king's throne name.

My name is Ozymandias, king of kings;
Look on my works, ye mighty, and despair!
Nothing beside remains. Round the decay
Of that colossal wreck, boundless and bare,
The lone and level sands stretch far away.

Topographically this is not accurate. Round the remains of the great statue are what is left of the Ramesseum itself, with wall reliefs showing the king's Asiatic campaigns, notably the battle with the Hittites at Kadesh which was the central experience in Ramesses' long life, judging by the number of times he had it depicted. The traveller today can sit in the shade of a spreading sycamore tree and look, in one direction, at cultivated land and, in the other, between pillars and ruined statues at the tawny hill of 'Abd el-Kurna where modern mud-brick dwellings stand among pocks that mark the tombs of viziers and other dignitaries long dead by the time Ramesses was alive and riding in his chariot at the head of an army, with the ram's head of Amon on top of a pole as witness to the god's presence.

A seat in the shade of that tree at the Ramesseum is as good a place as any to attempt some comparison between ancient and modern ways of thinking about the past. Greek and Roman travellers in the Nile valley enjoyed, as much as we do, the melancholy satisfaction of examining the broken relics of old glory. Unlike us they showed no sharp awareness that their own power was equally transitory. The examples of Greece and Rome provide the very evidence that gives depth to our own perceptions of history; whatever understanding we arrive at about the past is tinged with our European experience and expectation in a way that makes it impossible for us to write about alien cultures in, say, the jaunty style of Herodotus without appearing insensitive. Herodotus was not insensitive, but his anecdotes, about King Amasis, for example, who lived a life of pleasure and mocked the gods, have an almost vernal innocence. Amasis ruled on the very eve of the Persian conquest by the mad Cambyses in 525 BC. In the longer historical perspective the story told by Herodotus of how Amasis had a golden foot-bath transformed into the image of a god, so that he could mock the people who worshipped it, is no longer an anecdote but a cautionary tale. Herodotus saw Amasis in the light of morning; to us the time is later.

There is a wealth of evidence about ancient Egypt but we must not be overconfident about what we make of it. The wall reliefs of the temples, the reliefs and paintings in the tombs, the statues, the survival of letters, weapons, furniture, clothing, and even the bodies of kings, queens, and other notabilities, can create an illusory impression that we know this civilization intimately. The detail of life in ancient Egypt, particularly during this period of the New Kingdom, from the sixteenth to the eleventh centuries BC, is so available that people who believe in reincarnation have no difficulty in imagining a supposed previous existence there.

What really matters about a civilization is the inner life led by the people who created it, what values they lived by, what sense they had of the past, and what expectations they entertained of the future. The Greeks were the first foreigners really to try and understand the Egyptians; they made the most extraordinary mistakes, attributing to them wisdom and mysterious powers the Egyptians themselves would no doubt have been glad to possess but in fact did not. For our part we have to guard against a too facile understanding of a way of life that was different from our own chiefly in the way the divine and the natural were so inter-penetrated that there was no distinction between the sacred and the profane, where the annual rising of the Nile was understood as a manifestation of divine energy, where the king himself was a god, worshipped as such, and whose parent during the New Kingdom was the god Amon himself who, in the guise of the then living pharaoh, had fathered him on the queen.

One view of ancient Egypt is that from about 3200 BC onwards, when Upper and Lower Egypt were first united, the country enjoyed such continuity in its civilization there was little sense of change and development, certainly none of progress in the modern sense of the term. Life depended on the agricultural round. In an arid country that depended on the annual Nile flood and the depositing of fertile silt which the river brought from the Ethiopian mountains, there were only three seasons, of which one was the inundation. The need to control, conserve, and distribute water when the Nile had returned to its original course led to a highly organized and indeed bureaucratic society where everyone, nobles and high functionaries, priests, 'soldiers, scribes, artisans, and peasants, knew their place under the wearer of the two crowns, the king of Upper and Lower Egypt.

Unlike less fortunate peoples in Asia and other parts of Africa, the Egyptians were relatively secure from attack. Deserts to the east and west, the sea to the north, and a frontier to the south that could easily be defended against the primitive tribes that lived there made of Egypt a kind of island where a disproportionate amount of the national wealth was expended on tombs and other preparations for the next life. The military arts were neglected.

Egypt is not, however, an easy country to govern from any centre. Except in the Delta the habitable area is long and narrow. The distance from the mouth of the Nile in the north to Elephantine and the first Cataract in the south is over seven hundred miles, a three weeks' journey by boat, the normal means of transport. In the absence of a strong and vigorous wearer of the double crown, this straggling country had a tendency to revert to small, feuding states. The regime that built the pyramids came to an end in the twenty-second century BC in just this way and there was anarchy of a kind that caused one scribe to write, 'O that the country may cease crying out and that there be no more tumult.' His prayer was answered. A new order, the Middle Kingdom, followed, which was the great classical period of Egyptian history, when society as a whole was animated by a sense of probity and justice, and the Egyptian language itself was at the same time expressive and incisive in a way that meant all subsequent developments, no matter how much there was a gain in humanity, were a linguistic falling off.

Another period of confusion and uncertainty followed from roughly 1780 to 1560 BC. For all the appearance of stability in this most conservative of civilizations, a scholar of the New Kingdom like Amenophis, son of Hapu, who was so wise and learned that his memory was venerated for centuries after his death, could look back on good times and bad in a way that would disabuse him of any idea that Egypt was immune to change and disaster.

Nevertheless, it is doubtful whether he would have been capable of anything remotely like an apocalyptic vision of barbarians sweeping in, the ancient gods dispossessed, and power administered from somewhere outside the limits of the Nile valley. Amenophis, son of Hapu, had the records but nothing that corresponded to a modern sense of history. From his point of view, whatever aberrations there might have been in the past, there was also a basic rightness and justice about the ordering of the universe. Years of a 'good' Nile might indeed be followed by years of a 'bad' Nile when the inundation was too small to fertilize as much ground as was needed or so great that villages were washed away. But Kemi, the 'black land', was eternal. It imposed a way of life that was much the same whichever pharaoh reigned, whether he came from the north or the south, or even if he was a foreigner.

The exception was provided in the eighteenth century BC by foreigners known to history as the Hyksos. They stirred such hostility among the Egyptians that they inadvertently set this ancient, inward-looking people on a course of revenge and empire. There is still some uncertainty just who these Hyksos were. We hear of them from Manetho, an Egyptian priest and annalist living in Alexandria in the third century BC, who was understood by the Jewish historian Josephus to mean that Hyksos signified 'Shepherd Kings', and as such they have been popularly described ever since. In fact the name comes from the Egyptian words which may be transcribed as *hekau khasut* which means no more than 'princes of foreign countries'. They were not, that is to say, just pastoral tribesmen but a rather more formidable group of people, Canaanites in the main, who came down from Syria–Palestine – or Retenu, as the Egyptians called it – initially perhaps in search of grazing, or to trade, but at some stage quite definitely as warriors, with skills, particularly in the handling of horses and chariots, the Egyptians lacked.

At one time it was thought they invaded Egypt rather as the Normans invaded England in AD 1066 but it is now generally agreed that the Hyksos ascendancy was longer in the making. From time immemorial there had been trade between the Egyptian Delta and Retenu, particularly by sea with the ancient city of Byblos and by the donkey caravan routes of Sinai. A significant Asian population built up in the north-east Delta through quite unwarlike means, through commerce and the movement of nomads in search of grazing. This colonization was intensified by remoter pressures created by other migrant people. The second millenium BC was an era of considerable movement by whole peoples – Indo-Aryans coming into territories now forming part of Turkey, Iraq, and Syria, and putting pressure on existing populations, mainly Semitic, who were either taken over by the new military caste the Indo-Aryans provided or who began raiding themselves. In the confused period after the decline of the Middle Kingdom, the north-east Delta would be an obvious area for Canaanite adventurers to move into. A lot of the settled population there were their own kin.

From the upper 1700s BC onwards these 'princes of foreign countries' were able to assume political control of the north-east Delta with a fortified capital at Avaris on the Pelusiac, the eastern branch of the Nile. The ancient Egyptian divinity Set, the most potent deity in the area, was adopted and called Setekh; his great temple was rebuilt by a Hyksos king in 1720 BC. The site of Avaris has long been a matter of conjecture. Only since 1976 has excavation, carried out by the Austrian archaeologist, Dr Manfred Bietak, established that it is at Tel el-Daba, south of Qantir, and that the city possesses the largest Canaanite temple so far unearthed. During the more militaristic phase of the Hyksos colonization, Egyptian statues were defaced out of an apparent hostility to Egyptian culture. This evidence, found by Dr Bietak, is unexpected because it had previously been thought the Hyksos ruled Egypt, or parts of it, by adopting Egyptian ways. Perhaps the iconoclasm started with the Egyptian war of liberation.

Just how much of Egypt the Hyksos succeeded in controlling is controversial but their king, Sharek, ruled not from Avaris but from the ancient Egyptian capital of Memphis itself. The city is so placed that it commands both Lower and Upper Egypt. Sharek, therefore, was the effective direct ruler of the Delta and the indirect ruler of Upper Egypt through vassal princes, of whom the dynasty at Thebes was the most prominent. He also had an alliance with Kush, far away to the south, above the Second Cataract. This control of the whole country was maintained by Sharek's successors down to the time of Apophis 1, say 1650 BC. Although the alien regime was undoubtedly tyrannical and exploitative many Egyptians, particularly big landowners, saw advantage in collaboration – to secure grazing rights for their cattle, for example. It had long been the practice for southern cattle-raisers to fatten their herds in the Delta and this would have been impossible without Hyksos approval.

But Egyptian resentment of these alien top-dogs was inevitable. Who did they think they were? To the conservative Egyptian the normal role for these non-persons was as suppliant. But here they were as masters, speaking Egyptian in a way that was comical to hear, despising all the Egyptian gods except Set, and dressing ostentatiously. They were bearded, whereas all normal men were clean-shaven except at a time of mourning. They rode about in newfangled contraptions known as chariots – there was not even a proper Egyptian word for them – pulled by horses which, although not absolutely unknown in the Nile valley, were of less practical use than the good old donkey. They had bows made not just of wood but of wood, bone, and sinew, capable of shooting twice as far as the Egyptian simple bow. They exacted tribute and, perhaps worst of all, showed by their loud voices, not to say aggressive manner – when haggling over the price of a bale of linen, for example – that they thought the Egyptians were a lot of unenterprising peasants when they were not stuffy scribes, bigoted priests, or poor soldiers.

In Thebes the old virtues were preserved. Here, due reverence was paid to Amon, learning flourished, and in the arts the best was done with what remained after the Hyksos had cut off supplies of the traditional material, particularly cedar from Lebanon, and their allies in Kush had reduced the supply of incense, ivory, ostrich feathers, and gold. The Hyksos seemed to take pleasure in trying to humiliate Thebes. A papyrus fragment records that the Hyksos king, Apophis, demanded that the Theban prince, Seqenenre II, should give up his hippopotamus pool because the animals were making so much noise he could sleep neither by day nor by night even though he was hundreds of miles away. No doubt Apophis had taken pleasure in devising a demand calculated to humiliate Seqenenre and no doubt Seqenenre devised an elegantly artificial rejoinder – there was a code governing the exchange of challenges of this kind – though sadly we do not have the rest of the papyrus to tell us what it was.

Seqenenre died violently at about the age of thirty. The shattered skull of his mummy, which still survives, shows that he was clubbed or, more likely, axed to death and it is a fair surmise that this happened fighting the Hyksos. Thebes was the centre from which resistance to the Hyksos was organized. When the provocations became too much to bear, Seqenenre, in one of those sudden bursts of rage characteristic of Egyptians, probably committed himself to some premature engagement with the enemy only to be struck down. His body was recovered but not immediately; it had begun to decay before the embalmers could get to work. The implication is that the Egyptians fled from the battlefield and recovered the body, perhaps by negotiation, later.

The Egyptians had a lot to learn about fighting. At a time when body armour, the horse-drawn chariot, and the composite bow were used by their

Model soldiers from a Middle Kingdom tomb, showing the simple personal equipment of an Egyptian fighting force before it was modernized

Asiatic neighbours, and therefore by the Hyksos, the Egyptians were still dependent on the spear, the axe, the simple bow – usually of acacia wood and capable of an effective range of only about two hundred metres. If Seqenenre had worn a helmet, as his adversaries did, he might not have been killed. In Cairo Museum there are two troops of model soldiers taken from an Eleventh Dynasty tomb some four hundred years before Seqenenre but there is no reason to believe Egyptian military practices had changed much in that time and the models give a vivid idea of what an Egyptian fighting force looked like on the march before it was modernized.

Soldiers, naked but for short kilts, march four abreast, carrying long spears with bronze, leaf-shaped heads and large, highly-decorated shields. These shields, straight at the bottom and rounded up to a point at the top, were of wood and leather. No doubt they were heavy but they provided as much protection as could be devised for foot soldiers without helmet or body armour. The best they could manage in this respect were webbing bands over the shoulders and across the chest, together with the growing of a great mop of hair which may have been designed to provide some sort of protection for the skull. The bowmen are equally scantily dressed but what is of interest about them – apart from the fact that they carry arrows in their hands and have no quivers – is that they are not Egyptian but Nubian.

Nubian mercenaries came north in such numbers to serve the Theban kings, usually as bowmen, that they formed their own settlements. Their cemeteries were unusual because, unlike the Egyptians, they were buried in pan-shaped cavities, with the result that they were known to archaeologists as the Pan-Grave People before their identity was finally established. To this day Nubians are a tough, self-reliant people who do not normally intermarry with Egyptians. Their remote forebears provided an important and perhaps decisive element in the Egyptian fighting forces. The homeland of many of them was in the eastern desert between the First and Second Cataracts where, as nomadic tribesmen, they were known as the Medjay. It was by this name that they were referred to in the Theban army. Seqenenre's son and successor, Kamose, who carried on the war of liberation, attributed one of his earliest victories to these Medjay troops. The land of Kush, in alliance with the Hyksos, lay further south, above the Second Cataract, and produced an even tougher Nubian warrior, but in these early years of the war he was an enemy. Mercenaries from northern Nubia – Wawat, as it was called – were pitched against their Kushite cousins in the south; but the Medjay could only be trusted when they were not fighting a civil war and the subjugation of Kush, when it eventually came, was carried out by Egyptians.

In the third year of his reign Kamose told his council of advisers that it was intolerable to be sandwiched between one hostile foreigner in the north, the Hyksos king at Avaris, and another enemy in the south, the Nubian kingdom of Kush. He proposed vigorous action. He would slit open the belly of the Asiatic and deliver Egypt. All this comes from Kamose's own account recorded on stelae found at Karnak and if his council are reported as being unenthusiastic, this is probably because Kamose wished to emphasize the personal nature of his achievement. Egyptian kings did this throughout ancient history. Their advisers are represented as cautious, even timid men in need of vigorous leadership, which the king then provides. Kamose embarked a strong force on a flotilla of boats and was rowed north with the current of the Nile; his Medjay-Nubian archers stood on the roof of the cabins to be above the level of the banks so that they could spy out the flat land and give warning of ambush; a boy might be at the top of the mast in a basket to get an even better view.

Kamose had to fight Egyptian collaborators as well as 'base Asiatics'. By his own account he razed fortresses as far north as Avaris itself, though this is hard to believe; his real achievement was to destroy Hyksos power in Middle Egypt and that was achievement enough, for it prepared the way for the more ambitious campaign launched a few years later by the man who succeeded him, his brother Amosis.

Amosis had no illusions about the size of the task in front of him. Like his brother he would have been concerned by the inferior nature of the Egyptian weaponry and by the knowledge that the Hyksos were strongly established in fortified towns of which Avaris was only the most important. The high crenellated walls of these towns were further protected by a steep slope or glacis, making it well-nigh impossible to use the simple Egyptian battering ram, which was really nothing more than a long pole used to prod and prise apart the mud-brick fortifications. In spite of the importance of the Medjay bowmen, all decisive fighting was hand to hand. A lot depended, therefore, on the effectiveness of such stabbing, chopping, and clubbing weapons as Amosis had at his disposal. He was weak in chariotry and poorly supplied with horses, though once in the Delta the many water courses made it difficult to deploy chariotry anyway.

For all their skill in the practical arts the Egyptians were, curiously enough, never entirely confident about the casting of metal. Their axes were, as a consequence, usually less efficient than the Asiatic counterparts. The traditional Egyptian axe was a light weapon that consisted of a shallow, bronze, epsilon-shaped blade slotted into a wooden haft and secured by thongs. Something heavier was needed against an enemy wearing body armour. This was the eye axe, so called because its broader blade had two openings that looked like a pair of eyes. It was wielded with both hands. These two axes were for cutting but by the time of the Hyksos a third type had come into use – an axe with a narrow blade like a great beak that was used for piercing body armour and delivering deep wounds. It was probably with such an axe that Seqenenre was killed. An axe really needs a head with a socket into which the haft can be thrust; only in this way can it be made sufficiently robust. Such an axe had been used in Mesopotamia ever since the Sumerians developed it a thousand years earlier, but the Egyptians, either because they lacked the complex casting skill required or maybe out of unthinking conservatism, remained faithful to the tang, a back projection or projections of the blade that fitted into the handle.

The workshops of Thebes would be busy with the making of instruments of war, some of them – such as the chariot and the composite bow – being new so far as the Egyptians were concerned and imitated from the Hyksos. They both required considerable skill in the making and one can only speculate how Egyptians learned the craft. No doubt gear captured in battle was studied with

The temple complex at Karnak was the work over centuries of many pharaohs, and was the largest religious centre of the Ancient World
Opposite above : The Sacred Lake where Amon-re sailed in his barque and the sacred geese swam
Opposite below : The great obelisk and colossi placed by Ramesses II at the entrance of the Luxor temple

care and imitated. Bowsmiths, chariot-makers, and horse-trainers could have been bribed to come out of Retenu and set up as masters in 'free' Egypt. But however the skill to make them was acquired, the composite bow in the hands of Egyptians and the Medjay enhanced their fire-power dramatically. The different materials used in the making of the bow – wood, horn, tendons, and sinews – created more curvature, forming a double convex within the main part of the bow and then out again at the extremities, so that its elasticity and the strength needed to bend it were that much greater. The composite bow had something of the effect on warfare in the Bronze Age that gunpowder did in the Middle Ages.

A recruit needed special training to handle these bows. First he was taught the elements on a simple bow and then, after undergoing exercises to develop his muscles and being taught how to stand, he would graduate to the composite bow. On his left forearm he wore a leather guard for protection against the kick of the string. Practice at the range on wooden and sometimes copper targets was never-ending.

The chariot was an even more complex structure. The desirable qualities were lightness and strength. Ideally, different kinds of wood were required for different parts of the chariot; what was right for the body was not right for the pole that supports the body on the axle and runs up to the yoke between the two horses. Elm, birch, and pine found in later chariots would not have been available at Thebes because they originated in Retenu, so the best had to be made of local wood, acacia chiefly, and if need be old flagstaffs or door-posts were converted to chariot poles and spokes.

After the dawn service in the temple, Amosis took a light meal and went to the parade ground to watch young, brown Egyptians and black Nubians forming into phalanxes, marching and counter-marching behind fluttering pennants to the stammered command on trumpets. Hammers tinkled on bronze in the mud-brick workshops. The sound of saws cutting into wood rose like the thin whine of gnats. At the quayside troops practised embarking and disembarking under archery fire; other units from the Amon division were engaged on a mock assault with battering poles on an old building that had been transformed for training purposes into a fortification; under the protection of a structure with wooden walls and sides they stabbed away at the mud-brick wall while covering fire was provided by ranks of bowmen. Scaling ladders were used to get men over the wall, who then, in theory, opened the gates. In a real assault this was the time when the Scribe of the Army, standing at the king's right hand, would take down the name of any man who distinguished himself so that he could be rewarded by the Gold of Honour –

The hypostyle hall at Karnak. It was originally roofed over and into it the god Amon-Re would be carried in his sacred barque to make oracular pronouncements and receive tribute

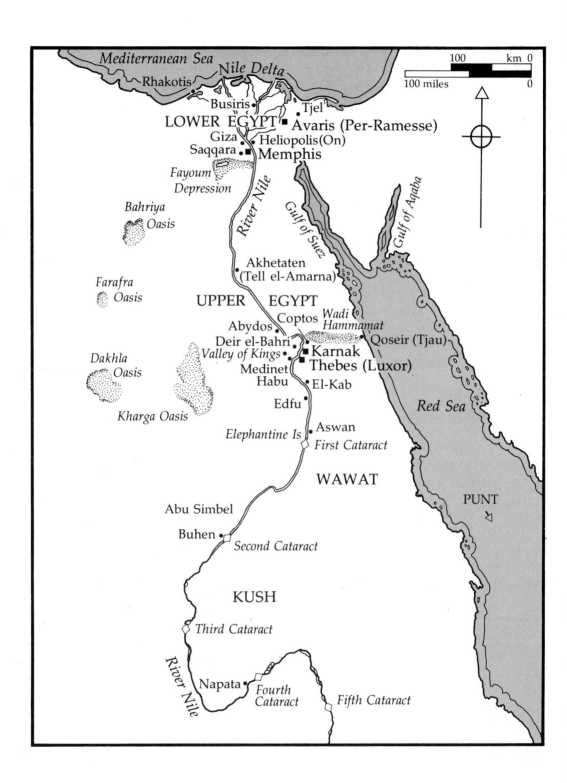

Mediterranean Sea

Nile Delta

Rhakotis

Busiris

Tjel

LOWER EGYPT ■ Avaris (Per-Ramesse)

Giza

Heliopolis(On)

Saqqara

Memphis

Fayoum
Depression

Bahriya
Oasis

River Nile

Gulf of Suez

Gulf of Aqaba

Akhetaten
(Tell el-Amarna)

Farafra
Oasis

UPPER EGYPT

Coptos

Wadi
Hammamat

Abydos

Deir el-Bahri

Qoseir (Tjau)

Dakhla
Oasis

Valley of Kings

Karnak

Medinet
Habu

Thebes (Luxor)

El-Kab

Red Sea

Kharga Oasis

Edfu

Elephantine Is

Aswan
First Cataract

WAWAT

PUNT

Abu Simbel

Buhen

Second Cataract

KUSH

Third Cataract

River Nile

Napata

Fourth
Cataract

Fifth Cataract

100   km 0

100 miles   0

gold flies or lions on a chain – by the king himself. If the garrison did not surrender, and sometimes even if they did, they were cut down with 'the edge of the sword', for before iron was used for weapons the long, thrusting sword was not feasible, and the bronze sword of the time was shaped rather like a sickle and used for slicing or chopping.

The god Amon himself would have signalled the start of the long campaign, lasting through many seasons, to drive the Hyksos out of Egypt. Concealed in his shrine, the cabin of his ceremonial boat, he rested under a canopy while contingents of the élite shock troops paraded. His instructions had already been mysteriously communicated to the king and were now pronounced by the Chief Priest: 'Utterance of Amon-Re, lord of Thebes. O my son, Nebpehtyre [Amosis], Lord of the Two Lands, I am thy father. I set terror in the northlands even unto Avaris and the Setyu [the Hyksos] are slain beneath thy feet.' The knowledge that Amon was committed to the destruction of the Asiatics who had killed the king's father would buoy everyone up with a sense of being the instruments of some divine vengeance. Egypt was old, had died as Osiris had been destroyed by Set (god of the Hyksos) only to rise again as the corn sprouted every springtime and as Egypt itself would flourish again. There was an outburst of patriotic fervour. The army was now referred to by the scribes and soldiers not, as was traditionally the way, as 'the King's army' but simply as 'our army', for it was fighting in a cause all could identify with.

The traditional view of what followed is that after some years of campaigning the Hyksos were defeated and driven out of Egypt. The Jewish historian Josephus, writing in the first century AD and making use of Manetho's account which is no longer available, claimed that something like a quarter of a million Semites left the country peaceably when Amosis, after failing to take Avaris, signed a treaty. But this is untrue.

One of the soldiers prominent in the campaign was Ahmose, son of Ebana, who came from El-Kab in southern Egypt. Inscribed in his tomb is the only record we have of what actually happened. King Amosis did indeed take Avaris, but only after set-backs; his near namesake speaks from the tomb: 'They sacked Avaris. I brought plunder from there: one man and three women – total, four heads. His Majesty gave them to me to be slaves.' It does not follow from this, nor from the account in the same tomb of the siege of a town called Sharuhen in southern Retenu with which King Amosis followed up his success in Egypt, that there was any mass flight or emigration on the scale mentioned by Josephus. Whatever happened to the Hyksos king, his entourage, his military commanders, and nobles the chances are that their former subjects, petty officials, estate managers, merchants, worshippers of Setekh, all would have remained. The charioteers, the horse-trainers, the bowmakers, fletchers, and armourers would be incorporated in the Egyptian war machine. And what did happen to the top people? There are literary reasons for believing that some of them may have gone as far as mainland Greece. According to Aeschylus (in his play *The Suppliants*), the heroic leader Danaus arrived from Egypt as a refugee but was not Egyptian; he could be the eponymous forefather of the Danaoi, or Greeks, of Homer and the other poets. Aeschylus did not invent the story. It was part of traditional knowledge that a man crossed the sea from Egypt to found a kingdom in the Argolid. This would fit what we know of Egyptian history at the time the Hyksos leaders were expelled.

Scarcely less important for the future than getting rid of the Hyksos was the way Amosis took a grip on Egypt itself and transformed it from a fairly loose confederation of baronial provinces or nomes into a more centralized state. Probably only a king who had waged a successful patriotic war could have been capable of establishing this ascendancy but even so the campaigns he now undertook into Palestine and into Nubia were not only necessary to secure Egypt against attack from those quarters but as a means of consolidating the king's power in Egypt itself.

In the course of his long reign of twenty-four or -five years, Amosis made himself master of the two kingdoms of Upper and Lower Egypt with greater power than any Egyptian monarch who preceded him. Barons and other top officials who gave evidence of unreliability, either by failing to send their sons to serve the king or by withholding manpower or supplies, were replaced by those more loyal. Outstanding service was rewarded by the grant of lands, and Ahmose, son of Ebana, who fought at Avaris and Sharuhen was one of those to benefit. Magnates who had ruled over vast estates and lost control of them were soothed with splendid titles, such as 'first king's son' and, like nobles under the French *ancien régime*, summoned to court where their activities could be observed. Almost single-handed Amosis created the basis for a centralized, military state which, when built on by his more famous successors, made the imperial age of Egypt possible. He founded a dynasty of which Tutankhamon two hundred years later was the last true member. Egypt was set on a course of expansion that led to a new internationalism and cosmopolitanism in the eastern Mediterranean as a whole and to cultural changes in Egypt itself. The new regime was certainly more authoritarian. One can only speculate about the extent to which this was willed. Amosis would have seen what he had done as no more than the circumstances required. Most of his subjects would want an end to troubles and see a strong monarch as a means to a more settled way of life. Once set in motion, the military and autocratic state followed a logic of its own and because the underlying policy that guided it was the policy of no less a being than Amon-Re himself, the priests who served him did so with an increasing sense of power.

2
EXTENDING THE
FRONTIERS OF EGYPT

UNDER AMOSIS THEBES WAS A MODEST
city compared with what it became later. Unlike Memphis four hundred
miles to the north, it had no ancient claim to be capital of the two kingdoms.
Memphis was the biggest city in Egypt and had been a great centre from the
beginning of Egyptian history. Its presiding deity was Ptah, who was represented as a mummified man with a staff not unlike Amon's; he had created
the world by thinking about it and giving utterance, a theological concept very
like the *logos* of Hellenistic times. No other place in Egypt provided such a
sense of continuity with the past as Ptah's Memphis. On the desert plateau
behind the city was the most ancient monumental stone structure in the world,
the Step Pyramid of Zoser, which was already over a thousand years old, surrounded by smaller pyramids and tombs and constituting a vast and still
growing necropolis. A few miles to the north were the Great Pyramids of
Giza themselves, scarcely less ancient than that of Zoser. In their sheathing
of fine white Tura limestone they shone like the rays of the sun pouring
through a rift in the clouds and petrifying hugely on the desert sand.

There were other ancient capitals. The city of On, later called Heliopolis,
was on the other side of the Nile to the north-east, so ancient that it was the
centre of a sun cult in prehistoric times. Much of Egypt had been ruled from
Herakleopolis, south of the Fayoum, until the ruling dynasty lost the struggle
with the rising power of Thebes in the middle of the twenty-first century BC.
The geographical position of Thebes, in a great fertile plain comparatively
easy to defend on the north and south, made it a naturally independent and
self-sufficient unit in a time of national disarray. Under Amosis the men of
Thebes could justifiably boast that they had never been militarily occupied,
not even by the Hyksos.

Most of the time the wind blew from the north and in summer its light airs
made the torrid valley easier to live in. The north wind was a minor deity not
only because of its cooling influence in summer but because it blew in the
opposite direction to the flow of the Nile. The ideogram for 'travelling north'
showed a boat with furled sails; 'travelling south' showed the boat with its
sail up. Even so, south-bound Nile boats usually needed more wind than their
large, square sails could catch and oarsmen had to help with the drive against

*Previous page : The Nile at Elephantine, the island which marked the
traditional southern limit of Egypt proper*

the current which creamed and chuckled under the bow.

To the north the limestone cliffs and hills, no matter how they retreat and advance towards the river, leave sizeable plains where barley and emmer wheat grow, right up as far as the Delta and its papyrus marshes. In the other direction, south of Thebes, the lips of the desert turn to sandstone and, on the east, rise sheer from the water. Before the island of Elephantine, where the king's barracks are, the fluvial plain widens again. Here, round the black, smooth, pachydermous rocks are eddies and whirlpools. Beyond, the river is splintered between long necks and rough hogs' backs of rock so hard that the current can only polish them, and crystalline so that the tiny facets flash in the sun; igneous rock, granite, gneiss, diorite, some red like the evening sun, some pink like Fayoum grapes but laced with a blackness like charcoal. To make the passage of boats possible through this, the First Cataract, the Twelfth Dynasty king, Senusret III, cleared a canal eighty metres long and ten metres wide. This is the end of Egypt proper.

Just south of here, at the height of the hot season before the inundation, a man's shadow was precisely between his legs, as it never was at Memphis, or even Thebes. In Egypt a man had a discernible shadow, no matter how small it might be, but here in Wawat a man could have no shadow at all worth mentioning because the sun stood straight overhead. Ahmose, son of Ebana, in addition to his other campaigns followed King Amosis on a punitive expedition into Nubia and he may well have theorized, being of an enquiring disposition, that the vertical rays of the sun had something to do with the amount of gold in the country. The strength of the sun is such that it penetrates the rock and changes it. The action of the sky-god, that is to say, is magical and when the ore is crushed to powder and swilled to and fro in water, the bright gold-dust that is separated out is the metal of Amon-Re in his solar aspect, incorruptible, unchangeable and eternal.

In Wawat the land was light brown, almost the colour of the Nile itself, and out of it rose hills of hard rock that might, in a certain light, have looked like pyramids. At times the river runs narrow and fast between granite gates and this is precisely the point of greatest danger because tribesmen can appear, loose off a volley of arrows, and disappear back to their caves before the Egyptians can respond effectively. Where the river broadens, sandbanks appear and shift so that a look-out with a long pole stands at the prow, probing the water from time to time. Because of the sandbanks the troop carriers were of shallow draft and light enough to be hauled through rapids at the end of ropes or even manhandled over the rocks. The men in command of these boats were not specialized water warriors but all-rounders like Ahmose, son of Ebana, who was proud to report how he had fought on foot in support of the king. But he regarded himself as an excellent marine too; he boasted how in an emergency he transported a king, not Amosis, from the Second Cataract back to Egypt by boat in record time.

Where the Nubian cliffs did not come down to the river, the desert did, bright yellow with sometimes, on the east bank, a village in a grove of palm trees and sycamores. As in Egypt the many-branched dom palm grew here, bearing nuts that were used to make a sweet drink. Yet mostly the land is desolate under its cloudless sky until, pressing still further south, the Second Cataract is reached where the river flows over greywacke and granite islets in a way that makes it impassable to boats. Here begins the land of Kush, the ancient enemy. From Kush came more gold, ivory, ostrich feathers, and, from remoter lands, negro slaves, and even dwarves.

In the past the fighting men of Kush had presented such a threat to the Egyptians that under the Twelfth Dynasty a chain of huge fortresses had been built in this desolate area to resist them. Buhen, on the west bank opposite present-day Wadi Halfa, was an elaborate structure with walls some eleven metres high, battlemented towers at each corner, outer and lower walls with semicircular bastions and a great protective moat all round. When the great gate with its double wooden doors was opened, the donkey caravans from the mines entered a sizeable town, with barracks for the soldiers, a governor's palace and a temple. The knowledge that Buhen and the many other fortresses of the Second Cataract area had fallen into the hands of hostile Kush during the Hyksos period must have been a source of resentment and apprehension to the princes of Thebes because they would have known with what

The fortress-city of Buhen at the Second Cataract. Originally built under the Middle Kingdom, it was restored and extended under the New Kingdom as a centre from which to govern Nubia

34

expense of national effort these remarkable examples of military architecture had been established. It was particularly provoking that Kush at this time was led by a dissident Egyptian, one Tetian; he had to be disposed of as quickly as possible.

Unlike Retenu, Nubia was regarded as a natural appendage of Egypt from ancient times and when, after we know not what skirmishes, King Amosis disembarked from his boat at the stone quay of Buhen and entered the fortress by one of the two river gates, he was displeased at the ruined state in which he found it and gave immediate orders for the reconstruction and extension of its fortifications. He appointed a trusted noble called Tjuroy to be commandant of Buhen, a successful appointment because he was eventually promoted to the new and important office of Viceroy of Kush in which he held court and dispensed justice in Buhen just as the king, his lord, did in Thebes itself. 'The King's son of Kush' or 'Overseer of southern lands' — variant titles for the Viceroy — was for a time the most powerful office under the crown. It only required the addition of a later honorary office, 'Fan Bearer on the King's Right Hand', to emphasize, with telling symbolism, the intimate relationship of power and trust between the king and his servant.

For all its remoteness and the dangers it presented, Nubia was a known quantity. Asia was not and the Egyptian expeditionary forces that went into Retenu found themselves in a strange land 'troubled with water, inaccessible because of the many trees, with its road bad because of the mountains'. Here were cities with walls not of mud-brick but stone; they had gates built in such a way that although chariots could drive straight in they had defence in depth provided by two or more sets of huge studded doors. No single monarch ruled over this land. One lot of people had control of the southern coastal plain, others the north, and up in the hills were tribes who fought one another and did not join forces even to resist the Egyptian invader. Plundering Beduin could turn up anywhere – 'miserable Asiatics', as one scribe described them, 'who do not live in a single place but his feet wander. He has been fighting since the beginning of time but he neither conquers nor is conquered. . . . He may plunder a lonely settlement, but he will not take a populous city.' This disunity and lack of order was an Egyptian advantage when, having scattered Hyksos strength, they pushed into Retenu to ensure it would never rise again.

In Phoenicia they marched up the coast road towards Byblos, a road so narrow between the cliff and the sea that at times there was room for only four fully laden spearmen to walk abreast. They marched on the beach itself, the waves of the almost tideless sea breaking deliciously over their feet. Inland, they marched through sweet-smelling birch groves and cedar forests. Fresh water came from the sky or in fierce, foaming rivers that rushed through deep gorges – so deep that the sun was glimpsed at the bottom only briefly – water so cold that men let it stand in bowls to warm before they drank it. To bathe in these icy rivers was unthinkable. One of them ran red in the springtime

35

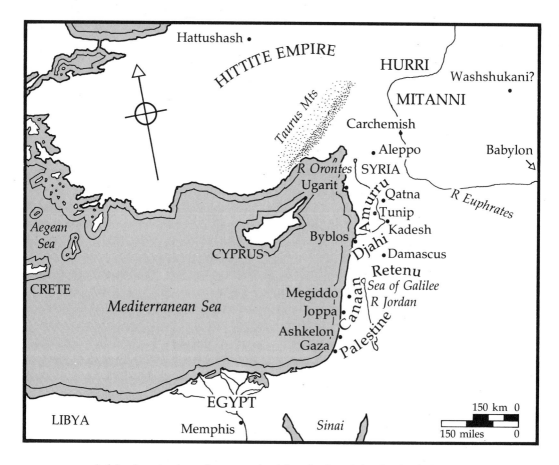

and this, it was thought, was the blood of a god who had died that the crops might grow, like Osiris. Bears came out of the mountains and stole food, even attacked men who had become separated from the main body. Snow stood on the peaks all the year round. Yet further north, in the flat land of marsh and tall grasses there were elephants!

There were also men who wore bronze caps and carried daggers so long they could pierce a man's body like an arrow. They spoke a flat, snappy sort of language, quite different from the deep, rounded sounds of Egyptian or even the throaty vocalizing of other Asiatics. In the main these men live in the land of Mitanni on the other side of the Euphrates, which was called the Upside-Down River because it flowed from north to south and boats put up sail to go downstream, the opposite of what happened in Egypt. These Hurrians talked differently because they had come down from some remote northland, near Mount Ararat, and had little in common with the other people in Retenu. There were strangers among them who were different again – a horse-breeding, aggressive race who fought from chariots and said they had come from where lapis-lazuli was found, in the highlands of the east.

Ahmose was a fairly common name in Upper Egypt. It means 'the moon is born' and its prevalence indicates a widespread moon cult of Khonsu thereabouts. In addition to the son of Ebana at El-Kab there was another Ahmose who served in Syria under King Amosis and eventually rose to high command in later reigns. He is known as Ahmose-Pennekheb to distinguish him. Such men as he brought back the campaign gossip to Thebes – about the way these Hurrians seemed to be in control not only of their own territory in Naharin, another name for the land of Mitanni, but they also had enough surplus fighting men to let them go off on adventures of their own, being paid by some city to defend it against wandering marauders only to take over themselves. The trouble was caused not by the Hurrians themselves but by their Indo-Aryan lords. In a way the disciplined and patriotic Ahmose-Pennekheb found hard to understand, Mitanni produced adventurers who seemed to have no loyalty to anyone; their ambition was to be rulers, no matter of how petty a state. They were known as *maryanna*, from an Indo-Aryan word *marya* meaning 'young man' or 'young warrior'. But they were all wretched Asiatics, Ahmose-Pennekheb would assure his friends back in Thebes, and presented no danger to Egypt. Less, certainly, than the Libyans.

The Libyans lived to the west of the Canopic branch of the Nile and in the deserts out beyond Fayoum, a semi-nomadic desert people who could turn up unexpectedly to raid anywhere between the Mediterranean and Memphis and even further south. They were brown-skinned, the men bearded, with tattoo marks on their arms and wearing penis-sheaths. They reared cattle and went in for agriculture in a half-hearted sort of way, planting barley and harvesting it but usually not in the same place for two years running, hunting gazelles and ostriches, and even trading with Nubia through the oases of Bahriya, Dakhla, and Kharga, perhaps for incense, ivory, precious woods, and pet monkeys which they bartered with merchants from Crete. Some of these Libyans had fair hair and blue eyes. It was well known that they had come across the Great Green from the 'Islands of the Sea'. They were a desperate, rootless sort of people who seemed to be increasing in number all the time. They could be a real danger to Egypt even though they were too poor to have anything but the simplest weapons. The fear of starvation made them dangerous. If they could get no grazing for their cattle they were liable to move into the north-west Delta in their thousands. What would be particularly dangerous would be collusion between them and the Nubians, which was by no means a fanciful fear.

Ahmose-Pennekheb did not think of the deserts where the Libyans lived, not even the oases, as part of the real Egypt. No sensible man would venture there except to punish and deter the Tehenu, which was the name under which he knew the nearest tribes. King Kamose, it is true, had sent a task force to the Bahriya oases to deal with Hyksos sympathizers. Amosis established a governorship of the oases but it was doubtful if the post was coveted. Life in the west was exile. Even less inviting was the eastern desert. In that waterless land of high mountains, marauding Beduin, goats, gazelles, pan-

*In contrast with the customary white garb of the Egyptians, desert
dwellers like these Semitic tribesmen wore brightly patterned clothing.
A copy by Nina Davis of a wall painting from a Middle Kingdom tomb*

thers, and eagles, there was no resting place. The only Egyptians who lived
there were conscripts and criminals sent to mine gold and quarry the hard,
dark stone the sculptors liked. Under the protection of the ithyphallic god
Min, traders and sailors travelled from Coptos on the Nile through the Wadi
Hammamat to the Red Sea; from the port of Tjau they could sail to Sinai for
copper and turquoise, or far away to the south, to the land of Punt where
incense came from. There were remoter lands. Lapis-lazuli, the colour of the
Nubian sky, most prized of stones, came from mountainous lands so far away,
in Afghanistan, that it had to pass through the hands of many traders before
it reached the Nile valley. From Sumer in lower Mesopotamia ships sailed to
India. About what lay beyond there was nothing but rumour, speculation,
and tall stories which were of no importance except as tales of wonder.

Richest of the islands of the Great Green Sea was Crete which had timber,
wine, oil, purple dye, and woven cloth. Cretan boats had sailed into Egyptian
harbours from what Ahmose-Pennekheb would regard as ancient times,

almost as long as Egyptian boats had sailed for Byblos. From Cyprus came copper. There was no certainty what the other northern landfalls might be, whether they were islands or parts of some greater country. Whoever the people might be who lived away from Egypt in these isles of the sea, in Babylon, Mitanni, Retenu, Nubia, or the western desert, they would all come to the 'Black Land' if they could. There was more gold in Egypt than the rest of the world put together and that was magnet enough; but the real attraction was the fertility of its black soil which did not depend on capricious rainfall and could provide food when elsewhere there was famine.

Ahmose-Pennekheb was no doubt a valiant soldier and all the more valiant because of the special horror Egyptians had of dying in foreign lands where, of necessity, duty now took him. Not only was he putting this life in jeopardy but, according to his deepest beliefs, the next life too. If killed in Syria there was no guarantee his body could be returned to his native land to be treated in all decency – after evisceration, the removal of the brain and other organs, it would be dehydrated with natron, embalmed, wrapped in linen bandages, and finally placed in a well-furnished tomb that had his achievements inscribed upon its walls. This was the only way to ensure immortality. The complete Egyptian world included territories entered only after death.

As it happens Ahmose-Pennekheb was interred as he wished. A man could achieve no more. Death was the doorway to another life which was thought to be very like the present one for ordinary men and women; for kings it might be different – Egyptians had the ability to believe contradictory propositions without undue strain – and the effective spirit of the dead, the *akh*, would be one with Osiris and live in the 'Field of Reeds' and the 'Field of Offerings', places of eternal blessedness. Another resting place was with the circumpolar stars that never set, that 'knew no destruction' but never wearied.

The king brought back to Egypt in record time by Ahmose, son of Ebana, was Amosis' son and successor, Amenophis I. During his reign (1550–1528 BC) the policy was deliberately formed of 'extending the frontiers of Egypt'. To realize this ambition the process started in the lifetime of his father was continued by Amenophis and Egypt became a military state with, for the first time, a large standing army officered throughout with full-time professional soldiers.

The Commander-in-Chief was the king himself and he led his army in battle. His right-hand man in military as in all other matters was the Vizier, who was personally appointed by the king. His was the greatest office under the crown. Its holder was responsible for law and order, the administration of justice, the organization of the economy, and, what is relevant here, the ministry of war. The Vizier presided over an army council made up of the most senior officers, men who had distinguished themselves not only by their sagacity and loyalty but on the field of battle. Wearing elaborate black wigs, pectoral decorations including the Gold of Honour, linen kilts, sandals, and – in cold weather – capes, they would sit on low, rush-seated chairs to discuss the training of recruits, weaponry, supplies, the reliability of mercenaries, and like subjects, all of which the Vizier reported to the king at his morning audience. On the field of battle the king would be advised by a camp Council of War whose recommendations he accepted or ignored as he thought fit.

For young, ambitious men the army was now the obvious path to wealth and power. Even boys walked in from the villages to volunteer. In the fullness of time they graduated from recruits to trained men and so to the *corps d'élite*, the shock troops who, like Ahmose-Pennekheb, fought near the king and were the first into the enemy town. Their sons became soldiers in their turn. Military families, with a history of service covering many generations, were the backbone of the armed forces and as such they formed a new and powerful class. Many high court officials came from their number.

Even so there were not enough volunteers to provide all the manpower needed. The population of Egypt at this time can be guessed at between three and four million, the great majority being workers on the land and their families. Agriculturalists are less ready to turn to the soldier's trade than migrant pastoralists or hunters are and conscription was necessary. A Scribe of Recruits in Thebes had under him officials throughout the country who kept a register of young men suitable for military service and when the need arose they were called up. The size of the standing army was never so great that conscription pressed hard on the population – perhaps no more than two or three per cent of eligible men actually served – but when the recruiting party came round they nevertheless had to be prepared to deal with weeping mothers and pleading fathers. Recruit training at Memphis or Thebes was not protracted. The aim was to blood the conscripts as soon as possible after they had mastered their weapon training. Together with volunteers and veterans they would sail south in companies of two hundred, each under the command of a Standard Bearer, ready to knock down Nubian strong points or charge Kushites from below the Third Cataract, fighting shoulder to shoulder with spear and javelin. The king himself, traditionally described as 'raging like a panther', would kill the enemy chief with the first arrow he fired – this is what Ahmose, son of Ebana, said – and then, if he was particularly barbaric, carry the body back to Thebes, hanging head down from the front of his boat.

An unenthusiastic and homesick recruit from some Delta village, who regarded his Standard Bearer and the enemy with almost equal fear, might be relieved the campaign had not been quite as punishing as expected. Anyway, he had survived. He had seen warriors blacker than a charred stick come suddenly out of the rocks with stabbing spears, screaming as they came. And he had seen them shot down by men the same shade of brown as he was, northerners far away from their native marshes. Back with the family a little boasting might be in order, particularly if accompanied by the handing over of a certain amount of booty – an ostrich egg, a feather, a drum, an ivory comb, even a gold ring or a panther skin still with the beast's claws and tail.

Amenophis was the first Egyptian king to set up the standard of Amon on the bank of the Euphrates and see rafts supported by inflated skins carrying cargoes of wood down to Babylon. Relations with Babylon were good. Amenophis may even have formed an alliance with the Kassite king who ruled there, for Egyptians and Babylonians had a common interest in containing aggressive Mitanni, the Assyrians, and the Hittites. Babylon was, apart from Egypt itself, the most stable part of the civilized world under its Kassites who, rather like the aristocracy who ruled Mitanni, were expert horsemen and charioteers. They had, perhaps, come originally from as far away as the Caucasus.

In Egypt a concept of empire had come into existence, its formulation aided no doubt by the oracular power of Amon. From the great bend of the Euphrates in the north to as far south as the Third Cataract in Kush, in the present-day Sudan, the king of Egypt was lord. In Asia he would not have seen himself ruling – as he did through his Viceroy in Kush – but it was his Amon-granted sphere of ascendancy whose princes defied him at their peril. The peoples of Asia were too varied and the land itself too difficult to police for there to be any question of establishing a 'King's Son of Retenu', a Viceroy who would administer the vast territory or even a part of it as a province. The possibility was no doubt considered and rejected by the god himself. The oracular pronouncements of a god were not just a mechanism whereby the king or the priests announced general policy or practical decisions. The will of a king such as Amenophis i was absolute but on such momentous matters as the 'frontiers of Egypt' it had to be related in some way to what was generally expected of the god, and this implied a significant broadening of the judgement. It was the less likely to be arbitrary. In great matters Egyptian kings were not capricious. Decisions were framed by reference to impersonal absolutes; in a theocratic state like ancient Egypt an oracle was the inevitable device for arriving at decisions all could be committed to, and as the empire developed Amon was called on more and more to act in this way.

So important was Amon in the making of state decisions, so vital was the part he played in the intimate life of the king himself, that the king can fairly be described as his surrogate even in the matrimonial bed. Amenophis's queen was officially known as the 'God's Wife of Amon', as his mother had been before her. Unlike any other ancient civilization, the Greek and Roman not excluded, the Egyptian gave women a status equal to men. They could inherit and own property in their own right; indeed it seems that property usually descended from mother to daughter. At the highest level of power they enjoyed special authority because it was believed that if royal they could be mated with the god, transmit divinity and therefore the kingship to a son.

They could even confer kingship on a non-royal husband. This is why so many royal marriages were incestuous. A king married his sister partly to stop somebody else from marrying her – and taking on the royal magic she could confer – and partly because it firmly established his own legitimacy. Queens had immense power in the Eighteenth Dynasty and some of them were remarkable women in their own right.

Tetisheri for one. She was a commoner. The fact is a reminder that for all the theory that kingship was transmitted through the female line and that the king's claim to the throne was strengthened by marriage to the preceding king's daughter, what repeatedly counted was the strength of the king's personal position. Unlike monarchs in Babylon, Mitanni, Assyria, the land of Hatti (where the Hittites lived, in Anatolia), the king of Egypt was not a man; he was a god and worshipped as such. His personal ascendancy was related in some mysterious way to the forces of nature, particularly the annual rising of the Nile, and the well-being of the nation. If he was a really strong figure who inspired unquestioned obedience in his palaces, his temples – for he was the supreme priest too – and in the army, he might not need the extra degree of legitimacy provided by a royal wife; divinity was the consequence of power in such circumstances, not the other way about.

This happened several times even in the New Kingdom, when the cult of the divine-king, son of Amon-Re, was a powerful political fiction. Without wishing to examine too closely the theological niceties of the position, the king would be aware that in addition to being the son of Amon-Re he was also the living Horus, the immensely ancient hawk-headed sun-god. The accretions of history threw up inconsistencies and contradictions out of which the propriety of a queen who was not royal by birth could be rationalized. The husband of Tetisheri ruled at Thebes during the Hyksos ascendancy but even so he evidently enjoyed the assured position that allowed him to carry off a commoner queen.

She was the mother of Seqenenre and would have seen his body with the axe-shattered head borne in on a litter. She outlived her grandson Kamose and survived long enough into the reign of her other grandson Amosis, one likes to think, to receive the messengers back in Thebes who brought the news of the taking of Avaris and the end of the Hyksos. In the British Museum there is a fine statuette of her as a young woman in which she is shown wearing a vulture head-dress with a *belle-époque* elegance; a delicate-featured woman with her head poised alertly forward on her long neck. Amosis was devoted to her and her memory. A conversation is recorded in which he declared his intention of giving her, in addition to her existing tomb at Thebes, a pyramid and funerary chapel at holy Abydos near the buried head of Osiris. The honouring of his family and particularly his grandmother (who was the

The limestone statuette of Queen Tetisheri as a young woman

mother of his mother as well as his father) was clearly of the greatest importance to Amosis. Tetisheri was plainly a great figure in the anti-Hyksos war.

An even greater heroine was Seqenenre's widow, the mother of Amosis, whose name was Ahhotpe. In circumstances that are still somewhat obscure she turned out the garrison of Thebes and put down a rebellion – perhaps on the death of her husband, perhaps on the death of her elder son Kamose – but in such a way, evidently, that stability was restored in Upper Egypt. She was certainly the dominant influence on Amosis early in his reign – it has even been suggested that she ruled jointly with him for some time. The wife of Amosis was Ahmose-Nefertiry who was of undoubted royal birth, perhaps even Amosis's own sister and therefore the daughter of the formidable Ahhotpe. It would correspond to what one senses of Ahhotpe's rather overpowering personality that she would want to see her own daughter as the only possible supplanter of her own ascendancy. That, it appears, was what happened when the old lady died, for Ahmose-Nefertiry was represented on the same scale as Amosis himself on a stela. According to the artistic conventions of the time this meant she was regarded with the same reverence as the king himself.

A woman could be queen in her own right and rule alone, like Queen Sebekneferu two hundred years previously. In the time of the military king and in the new heroic age that was dawning, a queen regnant would have encountered difficulties; the monarch really did have to be the man in the centre chariot on the battlefield. But the small-boned, almost bird-like 'God's Wives of Amon' during the early Eighteenth Dynasty were, in spite of their appearance, as tough minded as their kings and they exercised their undoubted power at a remove. It required only a small change in circumstances to make a woman the living Horus again. As it was, Ahmose-Nefertiri, who had a long life – well into the reign of her son Amenophis – achieved such popular acclaim as an influence in the highly successful consolidation of power at Thebes and as a public benefactor that long after she was dead quite ordinary people, the workmen in the necropolis on the west bank, worshipped her memory and asked for the consolations they felt she could still provide.

3
THE TUTHMOSIDS TO THE BATTLE OF MEGIDDO

To ensure that the kingship was transmitted to someone he approved of, the king could decide on his own successor, usually his own son, and appoint him co-regent. Amenophis I chose as a co-regent not a son – there is no record of his having one – but his younger sister's husband, a brilliant soldier called Tuthmosis. This was to be a famous name in Egyptian history not only because he made it so himself by his military exploits but because his grandson, Tuthmosis III, after a subdued beginning, rose to become the most vigorous and successful of pharaohs. If ancient Egypt can be said to have had its Napoleon he was Tuthmosis III, though as an exponent of an ancient form of chivalry he is more like Saladin. The designation 'Pharaoh', incidentally, as a synonym for king began to be used for the first time in this period. It comes from the Egyptian *Per-O* which means no more than 'Great House' and is a kind of metonymy like the Sublime Porte or Gate, used for the Ottoman court at Istanbul; or White House for the presidential machine in Washington. Pharaoh has become part of modern vocabulary because it is the title used in the Old Testament but, strictly speaking, its use for kings before the Tuthmosids is an anachronism.

General Tuthmosis, then, who became Tuthmosis I was almost certainly of royal lineage but what was of greater importance from the point of view of his claim to the kingship was his marriage to a princess of the blood royal, a daughter of King Amosis and Queen Ahmose-Nefertiry. He was forty when he came to the throne and a remarkable man. His first act was to send a despatch to Tjuroy, still Viceroy of Nubia, telling him to set up his coronation decree, which was to include the information that one of his titles, the Horus name, was 'Mighty Bull'. This was an innovation and it indicated his intention to be aggressive. Later the title would become standard even for less pugnacious monarchs. Within two years he had campaigned well to the south of the Third Cataract and finally destroyed the power of Kush. He hunted elephants in the marshy lowlands of the Orontes valley, somewhere west of

Previous page : One of two great obelisks of Queen Hatshepsut, which were erected a mere seven months after being quarried at Aswan. Her successor Tuthmosis III had them masked by a sandstone enclosing wall Opposite : Obelisks were holy objects in the Sun cult and usually built in pairs. The nearer of the two seen from the hypostyle hall of Karnak was erected by Tuthmosis I, the other by his daughter Hatshepsut

the present-day Aleppo, so relaxed and at ease was he in this northern and most hostile of the many territories that now paid tribute to him. From 'the Horns of the Earth', somewhere deep in the Sudan, to the marshes of Asia he was, in the language of the time, the sun-god who rose from the horizon and dazzled men's eyes when they presumed to look on him; and all this within fifty years of the destruction of Hyksos power. He was remarkable not only for these military achievements but because he realized that successful campaigning, which involved absences of some time abroad, depended on a loyal and efficient administration back home. This meant delegation of powers and Tuthmosis seemed to have the knack of knowing whom to delegate powers to. It was a key time in the evolution of the vizier system.

Thebes was now established as the capital of the new Egypt and its subject territories. Tuthmosis I was the first of many pharaohs to express this fact in monumental buildings there. His chief architect was Ineni, who is usually described as mayor of Thebes; this was a job in which he had responsibility not only for tax collection on grain but also for the upkeep of temples and it was in that capacity, under Tuthmosis' direction, that he planned the ambitious extensions to the temple of Amon. He could scarcely have foreseen that he was only the first of many builders charged to express the grandeur of the Egyptian state. The temple of Amon grew to be the largest religious structure for 'millions of years', as the Egyptians liked to say. With other associated temples dedicated to other deities, notably Amon's consort Mut and their moon-god son, Khonsu, at both Karnak and Luxor, the whole area became, with its obelisks, its sacred lakes, its stations of the god – where he could rest at some point in a procession – and its avenues of ram sphinxes, a holy metropolis where nevertheless private houses were packed and hovels festered against the very perimeter walls of the temples.

Towards the end of his reign Tuthmosis I could have disembarked from his state barge at the quay on the river bank and looked up to the two obelisks of red Aswan granite which Ineni had just set before the great gateway of the temple to mark an anniversary of his accession. The public appearance of the king was a splendid ceremonial occasion. Tuthmosis, crowned and carrying the ceremonial flail and sceptre, would be borne in his gold throne on long poles supported by bearers at such a height that the great fans to cool him and keep away the flies were on rods twice as tall as a man. The great gateway the procession now entered was the second to be built in his reign. On either side

There were many trading expeditions made to the land of Punt at the eastern end of the Red Sea. The best documented of them is Queen Hatshepsut's on the walls of her funerary temple at Deir el-Bahri. Opposite above : The queen's own boat (although she did not go on the expedition). Opposite below : Members of the expedition carrying olive branches and herbs

49

were broad, towering structures with façades that receded with height and having recesses where extraordinarily tall flagstaffs were placed so that their pennants could flutter over the very top of the pylons, as these gateways came to be called. The flagstaffs were tipped with gold, just as the obelisks had gold pyramidions on top to flash in the sun in a way that for the devout signalled the very presence of the sun-god himself.

Beyond the first pylon the king would enter a hall with a wooden roof supported by fourteen stone columns in the form of papyrus stems and calyces. The eastern wall of this painted reception area was an earlier pylon Ineni had built when it was thought the temple of Amon need extend no further, wrongly as it turned out when the king was sounded. Here, the great cedar gate of the pylon was covered with copper and bore 'the shadow of the god wrought in gold'. Beyond was a roofless court with a colonnade all round. Beyond that, as the king moved out of the sunlight, was the reception hall of the god, its roof supported by ornately carved sandstone columns. The only illumination came from quite small and high clerestory windows. On the other side of this hypostyle hall the level of the floor rose slightly and the roof came lower. Here was the unlit mystery of the sanctuary, with its supporting chapels and service chambers.

Just as under Augustus brick became marble in Rome at the beginning of its empire, so under Tuthmosis, in Thebes, wood became sandstone. This was the new, desirable, dark-brown stone from Gebel Silsila in Upper Egypt. It was used extensively from now on, for pillars in the hypostyle hall and for walls that were then covered with white plaster to be carved and painted in brilliant colours with scenes to glorify Amon and the conquering 'good god' himself, Tuthmosis.

The temple of Amon built for processions led by the king and High Priests out of brilliant sunshine through a succession of gateways, courts, and halls where the light progressively faded until they reached the total obscurity of holiness, was the pattern of most Egyptian temples to come. Tuthmosis might well have been satisfied with the achievement. The new Egypt had reestablished its cultural confidence. It is unlikely that he would have put this satisfaction in any historical perspective. But once, in classical times, long before the Hyksos came, there had been a more restrained expression in wood and stone of what it was felt the gods were capable of. Even their power, it was piously supposed, was limited. Here, in the 1520s BC, was the beginning of a new ostentation which seemed to imply that for Amon-Re all things were possible and it was in order to ask for them.

Ineni, mayor of Thebes, not only built greatly, he did Tuthmosis a quite different service: he found him an obscure burial place. 'In solitude, without being seen or heard', he supervised the digging of the king's tomb in a place so remote that the grave robbers would not find it. One wonders what happened to the workmen after their work was finished and Ineni had to be sure of their silence. The tomb of Tuthmosis I was the first in the Valley of the Kings. This winds into the edge of the escarpment on the western desert edge and was the burial place of Egyptian kings for the next four hundred years. His burial was made remotely and inconspicuously so that the treasure buried with the king might stand some chance of not being plundered; his funerary temple, where the rite of the dead king could be celebrated, and where no treasure was kept, Ineni placed elsewhere. This recognition of reality must have been painful. In theory the tomb of a dead king was inviolate because robbing it was sacrilege. In practice cupidity overrode, very often, fear of the supernatural and as a consequence the burial of kings became furtive.

Tuthmosis cannot have been much more than fifty when he died. His sons by 'the King's Great Wife' Queen Ahmose had predeceased him so he was succeeded by a son born to him by a secondary royal lady, Mutnefert, who may have been Queen Ahmose's younger sister. This son was Tuthmosis II. There was, however, a daughter of the marriage between Tuthmosis I and Queen Ahmose. The fact that she did not come to the throne herself indicates that in spite of the power royal women had, there was a great reluctance to see one of them actually wearing the double crown. She was married to her half-brother Tuthmosis II to fortify his legitimacy and so became 'the King's Great Wife'. Her name, and it is a famous one, was Hatshepsut. Like her forbears, the heroines of the war of national liberation, Tetisheri, Ahhotpe, and Ahmose-Nefertiry, she was a woman of considerable intelligence and great force of character – an even more decisive character, perhaps, than her young husband, Tuthmosis II.

Tuthmosis II seems to have been in some way deformed and he died prematurely, in his early thirties, but not before campaigning successfully in Palestine and Nubia. Of the two, the Nubian campaign was the more important. Kush as a serious military threat had been disposed of by his father but Tuthmosis II now had to deal with tribesmen who were out raiding for cattle and interfering with the trade routes along which passed ivory, ebony, and above all gold. The donkey caravans that plied from the valleys of eastern Nubia to the river ports were obviously vulnerable to the brigands who lived in this wilderness on dates and water. They would come charging down the side of the wadi in undisciplined ferocity and overwhelm the Egyptian guards by weight of numbers.

The uprising was not general, nor does it seem to have been directed in any unified way. A number of chieftains rose at roughly the same time, fortresses like Buhen were surrounded and anything that could be regarded as Egyptian property plundered. Like his father before him Tuthmosis II 'raged like a panther', sailed south with an army of foot-soldiers (chariots were useless in Nubia because of the terrain), and put down the rising with some ferocity. He brought back the son of a Nubian chieftain – to be educated, perhaps, and Egyptianized with a view to sending him back at some moment to take up a position of trust in his own country but with an Egyptian outlook. One of the prisoners Tuthmosis II took on his Palestine campaign was a young man who went through this process and eventually became a captain in the Egyptian navy. The policy of seizing young men from hostile territory, particularly if they were *maryanna* stock, and indoctrinating them in Egypt was much practised by Tuthmosis' successors. Tuthmosis II did not live long enough to wage the audacious campaigns his father did and, in a sense, the times did not require them. After two generations of warfare and plunder Egypt was, for the time being, sated. Even Amon seemed content, and this rather more relaxed outlook had much to do with the extraordinary developments of the next twenty years.

The death of Tuthmosis II led to an immediate crisis over the succession. He had no son by Hatshepsut – only a daughter, Neferure – but by a concubine called Isis he did have a son who may have been about ten years old when Tuthmosis died. Some forty years later this son, Tuthmosis III, told an extraordinary story about the way the god Amon chose him as king. He had apparently been intended for the priesthood and was being educated in the great temple Ineni had built for his grandfather. He had not, being so young, achieved even the order of priesthood, designated 'prophet' or 'god's servant'. On an occasion when his father, Tuthmosis II, was sacrificing to Amon in the temple, the boat shrine, with the god concealed within, was carried into the Hall of Cedar Columns where it made a circuit. Coming to where the child Tuthmosis was prostrate in adoration, the shrine halted. Gods had a way of making themselves unexpectedly heavy as a way of signalling they wanted to stop. Means were found on this occasion to raise the child to his feet and cause him to stand in the place usually reserved for the king himself. According to Tuthmosis III he was in this way made king by Amon during the lifetime of his father.

If this is true it meant that the reigning king and his advisers, including the Chief Priest of Amon, had formed the view that the boy Tuthmosis, the son of a mere concubine, should for state reasons be assured of the succession. They might even have believed that in forming this view they were inspired by the god. If that is so there would be no difficulty in the god taking action to make his decision known. No more dramatic way could have been devised of indicating that the young Tuthmosis was the elect of Amon than by halting the god's procession in his own temple and giving expression to his oracular powers in the presence of the most powerful in the land, including Hatshepsut herself as 'God's Wife of Amon'.

The general view nowadays is that the story is not true and that it was put about by Tuthmosis when at the height of his power to emphasize that in spite of his mother having been a mere concubine his legitimacy was unquestionable. But it is hard to dismiss the story as so much propaganda. The fact is that the boy did become Tuthmosis III on the death of his father and

Hatshepsut in male costume and wearing the war helmet kneels before Amon-Re

that could scarcely have been brought about without the kind of support the oracle had given voice to. The architect-mayor of Thebes, Ineni, was still alive and there is a record in his tomb of the manner in which he now responded to the death of Tuthmosis II.

Having ascended into heaven, he became united with the gods and his son [Tuthmosis III] being arisen in his place as king of the Two Lands, ruled upon the throne of his begetter.

While his [Tuthmosis II's] sister, the god's wife, Hatshepsut, governed the land and the Two Lands were under her control; people worked for her and Egypt bowed the head.

That is to say, when his father died Tuthmosis III succeeded him but since he was only a child his stepmother and aunt, Hatshepsut, acted as co-regent in name but regent in fact. He was probably married to Hatshepsut's daughter to give him the real status he needed to be pharaoh. Without the benefit of hindsight it is difficult to see an alternative course of action other than a regency under Hatshepsut until the boy came of age five or six years later at the age of sixteen. The priestly hierarchy of Amon, the Vizier, the army commanders, and the senior civil administrators would see it as a dispensation of Amon that the premature death of the pharaoh was not the misfortune it might otherwise have been. Hatshepsut was both the daughter and widow of kings. Were she to marry again (she cannot have been much more than thirty) her husband would have an even stronger claim to the throne than Tuthmosis but she never gave any indication that her thoughts might turn in that direction. Such men, then, as Hapuseneb, Chief Priest of Amon, Min-Nekht, the Chief of Works, and the venerable Ineni looked forward to the time when a woman would not be *de facto* head of state, when Tuthmosis III could come into his own and Queen Hatshepsut would retire with dignity.

Events did not develop that way. Hatshepsut decided that she liked power. It was intolerable for her to look forward to a time when, short of the tomb, she would have to surrender it, so in the second year of Tuthmosis III's reign she was, though a woman, declared king in her own right and it was as king of Upper and Lower Egypt that she ruled for the next twenty years. Tuthmosis III was not deposed, so the arrangement was in theory a kind of co-regency but there is no doubt that from the age of about twelve to thirty-two he was kept in the background and deeply resented the fact.

Hatshepsut is chiefly remembered today for her striking funerary temple built in a natural amphitheatre of the Theban hills at Deir el-Bahri under the supervision of her grand steward and favourite, Senenmut. What an Egyptian king chiefly took pride in – and she ruled as a king, even on occasion dressed as a man in short kilt and *hemes*, the horizontally striped head-dress – can be deduced from what he had inscribed on his temple walls. In contrast with other kings Hatshepsut showed scenes of peaceful activity. At Deir el-Bahri are scenes of an expedition she sent down the Red Sea to the land of Punt, probably present-day Somalia, to trade for incense, myrrh trees, ivory, ebony, and other products. The reporting is done with a great deal of vitality and some humour. The Egyptians could never resist a joke and the enormously fat wife of the local chief is shown with the animal on which she rides, a particularly small donkey. The scenes of the tropical countryside, the animals – including giraffes – and the huts on piles, in which the Puntites lived, are depicted with the kind of precision that could only be achieved by artists who had made the expedition for themselves and drawn from life. Only back in Thebes would the drawings be realized in stone. This was by no means a unique expedition. Trade with Punt had been carried on for centuries, by land and sea, but it suited Hatshepsut's purpose to emphasize that her father, the god Amon, had commanded it to procure incense for his ceremonies and ointment 'for his divine limbs'. Never before in state propaganda had there been such emphasis on the god's direction of national affairs. The Chief Priest of Amon, Hapuseneb, was also Vizier and therefore a figure of great power. It is reasonable to suppose that he was a key, or at least a compliant figure, in Hatshepsut's usurpation of the throne. Although she was strong, and probably a magnetic personality, she needed transcendental support. Amon, therefore, metaphorically speaking ceased to be hidden and came out into the light of day.

The king and queen of Punt. It has been suggested that she was suffering from elephantiasis

The god was also shown in the act of begetting her, with the kind of supporting detail that indicated Hatshepsut wanted no misunderstanding in the matter. In the form of Tuthmosis I Amon visited Queen Ahmose as she slept, waked her with his fragrance, and 'placed in her body' their daughter Hatshepsut. She was to be 'king of the whole land'. Amon, too, called for the setting up of four great obelisks at Karnak. Two of them are shown – so vast they needed a flotilla of twenty-seven boats, rowed by 864 oarsmen to tow the barge that transported them, a vessel one hundred metres long and thirty metres wide. We also see them erected, sixty metres tall and completely sheathed in gold, being dedicated to the god. Hatshepsut restored temples which, she claimed, had been neglected since the time of the Hyksos. In consolidating her own power she was incidentally providing the country with a breathing space in which domestic prosperity had an opportunity to grow.

This may have been the last time when a truly conservative point of view of Egypt's destiny was pressed with any confidence that it would be listened to. Are we not, the argument might have gone, in danger of ceasing to be

Egyptian? The language itself is being corrupted by foreign words. Asiatics are interbreeding with Egyptians and even rising to positions of power. What is the point of campaigning in foreign countries if the upshot is the importation of strange ways, strange beliefs and a luxurious way of life that is not in accordance with tradition?

Hatshepsut's favoured servant, the many-titled Senenmut, was a man of peace rather than of war. On the evidence that he secreted images of himself in Hatshepsut's temple and – an unheard of piece of presumption – dug his own tomb near its great court, it has been supposed he was the queen's lover. It seems unlikely. Hatshepsut gave him twenty high offices, including that of Steward of Amon, but she was much too interested in the maintenance of her power to risk having it threatened by an indiscretion. But that Senenmut's position was privileged there is no doubt. There are many statues showing him nursing the child, Neferure, Hatshepsut's daughter. He was not Vizier, he was not Chief Priest, yet he may have had more real power than Hapuseneb who held both these offices. The two men must have met and talked often, Senenmut perhaps putting the case for peace and stability and Hapuseneb, as befitted the priest, speaking of what Amon had become and would remain for ever, the god of war and the bringer of victory. This is speculation, but there could only have been tension between the two. Senenmut's position was anomalous. There were too many areas where power overlapped. How could the Chief Priest of Amon, who called himself 'Overseer of All Offices of the Estate of Amon', accept that the queen's favourite was also called Chief Steward of Amon, 'Overseer of the Granaries, Cattle, Gardens, Weavers', and heaven knew what other constituents of Amon's wealth?

The aggrandizement of Amon was a state necessity and his institutionalized power in the temple and its hierarchy was too great for the pretensions of a man like Senenmut whose power depended directly on the whim of the king-queen. He disappeared from history six years before she did and the portraits of him in his tomb were mutilated during her lifetime. The status of Amon as king of the gods was coincidentally being emphasized by accommodating other gods in chapels at Karnak, rather as a monarch gathers his subjects around him; and the Chief Priest became not only Chief Priest of Amon but a kind of *pontifex maximus*, Chief Priest under pharaoh of all the other cults in Egypt, including that of Re at Heliopolis and of Ptah at Memphis.

Tuthmosis III was a short, energetic man with a large, aquiline, but somewhat fleshy nose. He was level-headed, comparatively unostentatious but with great determination. His rather large brown eyes could stare long and hard. The accounts he gave of the various campaigns he fought are, in comparison with the usual bombastic utterances of warrior pharaohs, business-like and informative. He was a resourceful, imaginative general who showed himself magnanimous and merciful in victory; he had an appreciation of the arts, was reputed to have designed vases, jewellery, and temple furnishings, could compose hymns and write down wisdom, took an interest in the flora and fauna of the lands he campaigned in, and his devotion to Amon was such that the temple at Karnak received treasure, slaves, and the grant of cities and land in Egypt and Asia in greater measure than ever before. One of the un- answered questions about this period is how such a man could have been kept out of things by Hatshepsut until his early thirties. The vindictiveness with which after her death he authorized the destruction of her statues, the erasing from temple walls of her portraits and titles (replacing them, oddly, very often by those of Tuthmosis I and II), and the walling up of her obelisks seem un- characteristic of the man and must indicate the explosion of long pent-up feelings.

While Hatshepsut still lived, Tuthmosis concentrated his attention on the army, of which he was commander-in-chief. There can be no other explana- tion for the high pitch of efficiency at which the forces were maintained in spite of the prevailing peace. Early in 1468 BC Hatshepsut died, yet by the middle of April, Tuthmosis now having assumed sole power, he was already leading an army of twenty thousand men across the Sinai desert into Palestine on the first of his many and extraordinarily successful Asiatic campaigns. He called it, at the time, his first campaign, in clear anticipation of the many that were to follow; and they did, almost annually for twenty years. The speed at which he moved is surprising and surely argues that Hatshepsut died a natural death and there was no *coup*. After a *coup* there would have been a need for more clearing up, the elimination of possible dissidents, and the establishing of new, reliable functionaries, in a way that would not have been possible in a couple of months. Even before 1 February he must have known that the command of real power in Egypt, the army, was in his hands. There were no Hatshepsut adherents to plot against him.

Tuthmosis marched out of Egypt with rapidity because news had arrived that a confederation of Syrian princes was mustering under the leadership of the *maryanna* Durusha, prince of Kadesh, a key city on the upper Orontes, and had moved south into Palestine. This was revolt. The many city states of Retenu, with their racially mixed populations, had been regarded as vassals by the Egyptians ever since the time of Tuthmosis III's grandfather but years of Egyptian inactivity in the area had undoubtedly led to a strengthening of Mitannian influence. The danger of the present situation was that the Syrian princes had sunk their usual differences in an agreement to profit from what- ever political uncertainty there might be in Egypt as a result of Hatshepsut's death. Unless checked they might even march on the Delta.

A desert patriarch encamped with his family in the hills of Sinai could have looked west one morning during that spring of 1468 BC and seen the pharaoh's army as a cloud of dust moving north with the blue Mediterranean behind it. As the day progressed and the angle of light changed he would see the glint of chariots and spears. It was an army that intended to live off the land, one not so fat as Egypt no doubt but, in pockets, rich. Nevertheless, hundreds of trotting donkeys carried basic rations of bread, fruit, and oil to see them through to Gaza. A certain amount of water was carried in jars, though the army depended for its main supply on the wells that had been sunk along this already ancient military road for just this purpose. Tents, furniture, battering rams, spare poles, axles and wheels for the chariots, were packed either into the chariots themselves or tied on to the backs of the donkeys. Tuthmosis drove his own chariot. Attempts had been made over generations to make the desert road practicable for chariot traffic and a special effort had been made following Tuthmosis's own sortie against Gaza on an earlier, minor campaign during Hatshepsut's lifetime. But an impatient driver could end up with his chariot overturned and perhaps a broken axle. Hence the spares and the gear for a field workshop.

The army was marching into the land where the light chariot had evolved; the Egyptian words for 'chariot' and 'horse' were taken from the local Canaanite language. What was required of the chariot was speed, manoeuvrability, and stability at the pace of two galloping horses. At this time the wheel of the Egyptian chariot had only four spokes, which were too few for the battering it received. Later, the number would be doubled but this model lasted for such a short time before six spokes were decided on that it is possible to date New Kingdom engravings by the chariot wheels. The placing of the axle was crucial. The earliest Mesopotamian chariots were heavy, trundling vehicles with the axle about half way between the front and the back of the body, but as time went by it was placed further and further to the rear as a means of increasing stability. The chariots of Tuthmosis III had not quite realized the ideal position, which was for the axle to be flush with the rear of the body. The car itself was little more than a wooden frame covered with leather or basketwork. Here, on its small platform, was just room for two men to stand, the charioteer and the warrior who was armed with a shield, a composite bow, a javelin, and probably a short sword.

Nobody thought of fighting on horseback though messengers sometimes travelled in this way. There were a number of reasons for this. The horse of the time may not have been robust enough; riding was in any case thought by the Egyptians to be undignified; and thirdly, the warrior of the time needed a firm place to stand from which he could fire arrows, hurl a javelin or swing his short sword or mace. The chariot provided such a place but in the absence of stirrups the horseman had an insecure seat and could easily be dismounted. Stirrups, which made cavalry possible, did not come into use

Opposite : Senenmut, Queen Hatshepsut's favourite minister, holding the princess, Neferure
Overleaf : Hatshepsut's funerary temple built in an amphitheatre of the Theban hills

until a couple of thousand years later; Alexander the Great had no really effective cavalry, nor did the Romans.

The chariotry enjoyed all the prestige that in later armies was attached to the cavalry and was organized in squadrons of twenty-five, commanded by a 'Charioteer of the Residence' who in turn came under the 'Lieutenant-Commander of Chariotry'. A position of particular glory was that of 'First Charioteer to His Majesty' though, on the march, Tuthmosis may well have dispensed with his services. The firm earth of the coastal plains and inland valleys of Retenu provided better chariot country than the sand of Egypt, particularly now that the winter rains were over, and Tuthmosis would have enjoyed the luxury of wheeling back along the line of march and giving encouragement to the troops.

Standard Bearers marched before their regiments bearing ensigns of a form and colour that could readily be picked out in the murk of battle and serve as rallying points, some in the form of fans bearing the king's name, others looking like flails. Each division was a complete army corps, five thousand strong, made up of chariotry, the various kinds of infantry and bowmen with the associated supply troops, scribes, and artisans. On this particular campaign a scribe called Tjaneni kept a military diary which eventually became the basis for the official account as displayed on the temple walls back in Thebes.

Many of these troops had come from well south of Memphis and the recruits among them had never seen such big-bellied clouds. After covering the 150 miles from the Egyptian frontier fortress of Tjel to Gaza in ten days, they now marched through palm groves and fields of newly springing wheat. From Gaza north to the Carmel ridge that shuts off the coastal plain of Palestine from the Plain of Esdraelon, and the possibility of all further progress north, is a further eighty miles, which were covered in eleven days. There is a tradition, preserved in a popular story of late pharaonic times, that the walled city of Joppa was taken by a trick; Egyptian soldiers were conveyed into the city not in a wooden horse but in sacks and baskets which the besieged thought contained tribute from the surrendering Egyptian commander.

Before the middle of May Tuthmosis was encamped at Yehem just south of the Carmel ridge with a choice of three passes to negotiate before he could reach the strongly fortified city of Megiddo, where the prince of Kadesh and his allies were waiting for him. The speed of Tuthmosis's response must have startled them. Even so, there being a certain formality in the waging of war

The mountains, torrents, and forests of Lebanon and Syria were a strange and alarming world for the invading Egyptians. Opposite above : The mound beyond the Orontes is the site of Kadesh, long the centre of resistance to Egyptian imperialism. Ramesses II's battle with the Hittites took place on the west bank of the river. Opposite below : The Adonis river or Nahr Ibrahim flowing down from the heights of Mount Lebanon

63

The Sinai desert, Egypt's eastern frontier across which her armies marched along the military road into Asia

in those days, Durusha let it be known that he would stay where he was and await the Egyptian attack.

At Yehem, Tuthmosis called a council of war. The question before him and his senior officers was which of those alternative routes to take. Two routes, the northerly and the southerly, would allow an orthodox approach to Megiddo, the army marching as an army, with scouts on the surrounding hills. The central, more direct route was so narrow that at points the army would have to proceed in single file, man behind man, horse behind horse, chariots lifted – perhaps even carried for some distance – over the stones. This council of war is one of two we know about conducted by pharaohs in the field (the other was 168 years later when Ramesses II called one at Kadesh) and no doubt was standard practice before a major engagement. Such councils were also reported in a way to reflect as favourably as possible on the pharaoh's judgement.

There was no question of taking a majority vote or even arriving at a consensus. Pharaoh would listen to the views of his officers and make up his own mind – at least, that is the way one can be certain Tuthmosis III operated. To succeed, a council of this kind must be based on the knowledge that every man knew the exact limits of his authority but nevertheless was under an obligation to speak fearlessly. In normal circumstances, and probably even at the Yehem council, no one would presume to address pharaoh directly, but only to 'speak in his presence'. The authority of Tuthmosis himself, the 'good god', 'beloved of Re, son of Amon', was limitless in theory but in practice a military leader who overrode the united and strong views of his council would be asking for trouble. This, according to the account on the temple wall, is just what Tuthmosis did.

64

The council argued that the direct route to Megiddo, through the pass of Aruna, was too dangerous. Even if they were not ambushed, which was highly likely, the vanguard of the army would emerge at the other end of the pass and be engaged by the enemy in strength while the rest of the Egyptian army, strung out over a distance of some miles, would be still coming through and quite unable to give any assistance. Tuthmosis would have none of this. 'I will take the Aruna road. If you want to go by one of these other routes you may do so, but those who want to follow me are free to do so also. If I were to act otherwise what would these fallen men of Kadesh think, these men whom God holds in horror? His Majesty is afraid of us. That is what they would think.'

Tuthmosis did not actually command his officers to follow him through the pass of Aruna and the account gives the impression that he would have gone alone if necessary. The council had, of course, no alternative but to declare immediately that they would follow the king wherever he went. 'Your father, the god Amon, will bring about the fulfilment of your Majesty's intentions,' they declared. They, the council, were but His Majesty's servants and they had no will but that of His Majesty. Having assumed total responsibility under Amon for the course to be followed Tuthmosis now announced that he himself would be at the head of the column through Aruna and they would be moving at first light.

The prince of Kadesh had meanwhile concentrated his forces near Taanach at the eastern end of the southern route over the Carmel ridge. Had Tuthmosis taken that route he would have fought a battle on ground of their choosing. Had he taken the northern route, a considerable detour, he would have given the Syrians time to redeploy. By unexpectedly taking the shorter, more direct and difficult middle route Tuthmosis could, assuming he reached the valley on the other side with his army intact, establish himself on the enemy's right flank. They would then have to redeploy in a hurry. Instead of fighting at Taanach from well-prepared positions the Syrians would now have to fight on ground of Tuthmosis' choosing. And this is what happened. If he knew, from intelligence supplied by his scouts, that the Syrians were at Taanach then Tuthmosis is the first commander in history who can be credited with the ability to marshal the constituent parts of his army, the divisions, to the point of tactical advantage where the flank of the army was turned and the enemy could be caught at that moment of disadvantage when redeploying to meet this unexpected threat. If he did not know where the Syrians were, then he had that other necessary quality for the great commander, luck.

It took about twelve hours to get the whole army through the Aruna pass. At the suggestion of his council, Tuthmosis himself waited at its eastern end for the rearguard. This was a tactful way of ensuring that he did not attack prematurely, as they feared in his impetuosity he might. Then the army camped for the night. The reaction of the Syrians can only have been one of surprise and dismay. They had nothing like the unity of command the Egyptians enjoyed; their forces were made up of what a great many semi-autonomous barons could provide, a great gathering of private armies some of which may have amounted to no more than a single chariot and half a dozen infantry. Their move to take up position opposite the Egyptian army seems not to have been well executed and possibly there was recrimination between the different leaders about the surprising failure to place a precautionary force at Aruna where at the least it could have held Tuthmosis up.

The Syrians could not see the Egyptians and the Egyptians could not see them. The thin sliver of the new moon was a particularly favourable omen, for the family of Tuthmosis enjoyed the special favour of the moon-goddess. Being pharaoh and of necessity somewhat aloof – an earlier king had told his son that one of the prices of kingship was loneliness – Tuthmosis cannot be imagined with that common touch which, like Henry v before Agincourt, would have caused him to move among his troops and hearten them for what daylight would bring. He would have made sacrifices to Amon and to the falcon-headed Montu, god of battles, and then retired to his tent with instructions to the guard that he be awakened at the darkest hour. If he dreamed it could have been that Hatshepsut was strangling him. But when he awoke, sweating, it was in the knowledge that she was dead and he was free.

On higher ground than the enemy Tuthmosis could look over them straight into the rising sun. The Egyptian right wing of foot soldiers and archers was extended south and west to a small hill on the other side of a brook called Kina; the left wing stretched north and west to a point near Megiddo itself, which stood behind stone walls on a hill. The centre, where the chariotry was concentrated, was commanded by Tuthmosis himself and he displayed himself like a god, 'in a chariot of fine gold, adorned with his accoutrements of combat, like Horus, the Mighty of Arm, a lord of action like the war-god Montu, the Theban, while his father Amon made strong his arms'. One can imagine that this small man in a blue leather crown which served as a helmet, raised up in the bright light not much more than six hundred metres away, looked almost supernatural to the Syrians. The royal uraeus serpent on his forehead spat fire. Trumpets sounded, troops rattled their weapons on their shields, and Tuthmosis gave the order to advance down the slope to a point where the enemy were within bow range. There was not such a plentiful supply of arrows that any could be wasted.

The Egyptians claimed that the forces of Kadesh were enormous – 330 kings, millions of infantry, and hundreds of thousands standing in their chariots. This is the usual hyperbole. But at the first flight of arrows, at the first charge of the chariots, the Syrians who were still moving to take up position and at a hopeless disadvantage seem to have been so demoralized that they broke and ran for Megiddo, where the gates were shut against them.

The prince of Kadesh and his vassal the lord of Megiddo had to be hauled up the walls with great loss of dignity by ropes made of clothing, much to the delighted amusement of the Egyptians. But at this point Tuthmosis lost control of his army.

Instead of following up the advantage and driving straight for Megiddo, which might have fallen, the Egyptians fell to plundering the camp of their enemies. Tuthmosis laid siege to the city, saying: 'Every prince of every northern country is shut up within it; so the capturing of Megiddo is the capturing of a thousand towns.' With the expenditure of a prodigious amount of effort the Egyptians now encircled the city with a moat and a wooden palisade to make sure no one left except to surrender. The siege lasted for seven months and while it went on Tuthmosis raided east to the region of Lake Galilee where the prince of Kadesh had an estate to which he had sent his family for safety. Another great raid was up to the Mediterranean coast north of Byblos and then east again, over the Lebanon range and the central Beka'a valley to Damascus, which was seized. Hazor, one of the great cities of Syria, seems to have been visited though it is unlikely so well-fortified a place could have been taken in the short time available. With the Syrians shut up in Megiddo the Egyptians were able to roam their territory as they willed.

In December the city surrendered and Tuthmosis, with a restraint and far-sightedness unusual for the time, took no lives. Some of the Syrian leaders seem to have been taken back as hostages to Egypt but for the most part they were returned to their respective cities, after taking oaths of allegiance, riding on donkeys – donkeys because Tuthmosis wanted their horses, nearly two and a half thousand of them. Durusha, prince of Kadesh, himself managed to escape.

Like Saladin's magnanimity to the Christian inhabitants of Jerusalem when he took the city in AD 1187, Tuthmosis' restraint had political consequences. Nothing stiffens the resolve of a besieged city more than the knowledge that its fall will lead to wholesale massacre. Tuthmosis' humane policy probably contributed to the effectiveness of the control Egypt was able to exert in this part of the world for such a considerable period of time; in some measure he was able, through his clemency, to enlist the respect and loyalty of the rulers of Retenu, so that his successors right down to the time of Akhenaten a hundred years later could count on the support of some of them in any time of trouble. His triumph was complete. The princes of the conquered territory had taken oaths of loyalty, they had acknowledged an obligation to pay tribute and now, after appointing resident governors such as General Djehuty, the man supposedly responsible for the trick that took Joppa, he returned to Egypt after an absence of nearly a year.

Tuthmosis would have been kept in touch with domestic affairs by the Viziers. At one time a single Vizier had sufficed as the king's chief minister

67

throughout the two lands but now – in addition to the Viceroy of Nubia – the new *dirigisme* required two Viziers, one based at Thebes for Upper Egypt and the other at Memphis for Lower Egypt. When the king was resident at either of these two centres the Vizier reported to him every day and received instructions. In campaign time some effective substitute for the daily audience had to be contrived and although a daily despatch was too much to expect nevertheless a good many couriers were kept busy, with wallets containing papyrus despatches suspended from the neck by a leather strap. They travelled in fast, light carriages called *merkobt*, which were variants of the chariot, drawn by two horses and with a guard. At intervals there were posting stations where horses and, if necessary, the *merkobt*, could be changed.

The Viziers ran Egypt, not only when the king was campaigning but when he was at home which, in the case of Tuthmosis III, was not all that often in the early part of his reign. It was a job that called for high administrative ability and loyalty, and evidently these qualities were considered to run in families. Ahmose, called Amotju, Amenwosre, and Rekhmire, who were all Viziers at Thebes in the time of Hatshepsut and Tuthmosis III, were related and there was a fourth member of the family, Neferweben, who was Vizier at Memphis. Officials liked to describe how pharaoh had raised them from obscurity and examples are known of prominent men, at this time of an emerging new meritocracy, who came from a peasant background. But that was exceptional. The vizierate demanded such a combination of qualities, trustworthiness not being the least of them, that pharaoh would not wish to take risks. Family tradition would have counted for a great deal and there was a general expectation that jobs were hereditary. The Vizier of the south at the time of Tuthmosis's first Asiatic campaign was Amotju. There is some reason to believe that he was unhappy with the Hatshepsut regime and was accordingly dismissed, only to be reinstated by Tuthmosis. This crucial reappointment must have been decided upon in the short period between Tuthmosis's accession at the beginning of 1468 BC and his departure for Retenu.

The job of Vizier was onerous. In the words of the king uttered on his appointment: 'The position of a Vizier is not pleasant at all; no, it is bitter as gall.' The king himself was the only law-maker and decider of important initiatives but the Vizier was answerable to him for security, for the administration of justice, the gathering of taxes, the receiving of foreign envoys and foreign tribute, for the land survey particularly after the annual flooding of the Nile when new boundary marks would be set up, irrigation canals dug and forced labour (*corvée*) exacted. The list is never-ending, down to such detail as the felling of sycamore trees. No doubt these responsibilities were carried out by delegation but even so the Hall of the Vizier was, in the words of the king, 'the consolidation of the whole land' and the holder of that office must have experienced the stresses in society, both potential and actual, in a quite personal way.

Tuthmosis III in the traditional pose of pharaoh symbolically sacrificing foreign prisoners to Amon-Re

All the more important, the king said, for the Vizier to be just in all his dealings, without fear or favour. 'Give as much attention to the man you know as to the man you do not know, no more to he who approaches you in person than to one who is far away.' Give reasons for all decisions. 'Do not be angry with a man unfairly, but only with due cause.' Inspire a proper fear but not to a point people think it interferes with honest dealing. Indeed, the ideal is honest-dealing in all matters, in accordance with the ancient virtues of truth, justice and order, the word for which was *Ma'at*. In the tomb of Rekhmire there is a representation of the Vizier sitting as Chief Justice with prisoners and litigants before him. Before his chair of office lie forty objects in groups of ten on four mats. They may be leather thongs for punishment, rods of office or, what is commonly supposed, scrolls of the law. There is no firm evidence for a codification of Egyptian law though the tomb inscriptions particularly refer to the Vizier having access to records of all legal decisions. It would be surprising if so systematic a people had no legal code and expected the Vizier to work only from case law and first principles.

The Vizier's job description and the royal guidance on his conduct as set out in these tombs had a long history behind them but there is no doubt they indicate what actually went on under Tuthmosis III. On his triumphant return from Syria he would once more take up his granting of daily morning audience to the Vizier Amotju in the palace at Thebes – a palace that was not just a royal residence but the administrative centre for the whole country. He would want detailed reports on the state of the land, arrangements made for the allocation of war booty to the great temples, particularly the temple of Amon, new plans for the levying of troops put forward, instructions for the enlargement of the dockyard at Memphis, and the expansion of the navy carried out; and, perhaps, the view was communicated that Amotju was doing too

69

much work for one man. He must delegate more to his scribes, heralds, and deputies, otherwise he would be prematurely occupying the splendid tomb on the west bank the Vizier already had in hand. The Vizier's traditional greeting to the king would be: 'Life, prosperity and health to Your Majesty. All Your Majesty's affairs are in good order. Every official on duty reports that all is safe and sound.' To which vague assurances Tuthmosis, being Tuthmosis, would respond: 'Amon be thanked but why is the irrigated area in the Hare nome so much less than last year?' Or some such question on detail.

On his return from the first of his seventeen campaigns Tuthmosis ordered a victory feast which lasted five days. There was a great distribution of food and beer, the king repeatedly appeared at the palace window to throw down gold necklaces, bracelets and other gifts to the favoured ones. He publicly awarded the Gold of Honour to those who, for some reason had not, in accordance with normal custom, received it on the battlefield.

His first encounter with the god Amon after such a long absence would be a particularly solemn occasion. Purification was no mere ritual. The two priests, according to prevailing belief, really did purify him, one wearing an ibis mask to simulate the god Thoth, the other a hawk mask to simulate Horus. They sprinkled the god with holy water, burned incense, and gave him a pellet of natron to chew and so make his mouth clean for the uttering of his holy address to Amon; Tuthmosis would feel that grossness had been purged away. After the ceremony in the small chapel known as 'The House of Morning' he approached the Holy of Holies with the Chief Priest in attendance. In the silence and darkness he seemingly heard again the grinding of chariot wheels, the twang of arrows, the crash of onset, and the cries of the wounded. Tuthmosis himself opened the wooden doors of the shrine and saw, by the light of oil lamps, the face of his father. With the god reverently placed on a hillock of sand before his boat shrine, the king intoned the hymn and performed the service – purification, dressing, toilet, and the offering of the divine banquet. The relationship between the god and Tuthmosis provided the sanction for everything he, as pharaoh, did. For him there was in this world no profounder reality.

At the end of the morning service, the king performed the ceremony of retiring. The god went back to his granite shrine, the doors were closed and sealed with a clay seal; and, as the king withdrew from the sanctuary he swept the sanded floor with a broom to obliterate his footprints. There is no reason to suppose that for Tuthmosis the renewal of his daily encounter with the god had been anything but profoundly moving. On the campaign he had been sustained by a small Amon-of-the-Roads in a portable shrine but to see the god in his temple was, to use Tuthmosis's own words on another occasion, 'for the doors of heaven to open and myself flying to heaven as a divine hawk to see the mysterious form of god himself'.

4
HEROES AND
CONQUERORS

THE FIGHTING PHARAOHS HAD NO
high-minded view of what they were up to. Other empires had ideologies.
Alexander, by implication, aimed at a new kind of internationalism. The
Romans were self-conscious about their civilizing mission, the Arabs fought
under a religious imperative, and modern empires, like the British, were
formed out of some cloudy idea of doing good. The ancient Egyptians may
have been smug about their cultural inheritance but they were entirely lacking in the kind of moral earnestness that would have caused them to impose
their own values and institutions in Asia.

In Nubia, yes. Nubia was different. Nubia was part of the Nile valley, it was
a traditional area of Egyptian influence and dominance. From the Egyptian
point of view the sooner all Nubians worshipped Egyptian gods, particularly
Amon, the sooner they would emerge from the tribal barbarism in which they
languished. The transformation of a once independent Nubia into an appendage of Egypt was part of the struggle not between man and man but of some
less personal battle, for control of the environment. The Egyptians just had
to be masters of the land the Nile came from. If all the provinces of Asia were
swallowed by the primeval serpent Neheb-kau and never regurgitated, Egypt
would carry on as before; but if the serpent took Nubia the Nile itself would go.

In Asia the Egyptians recognized no mission but to exploit it. Such commissars as the General Djehuty were known as 'Overseers of all Northern
Countries'. Their main job was to ensure that the vassal princes and chieftains paid their annual tribute and, when pharaoh appeared in their country,
were in the appropriate state of awe to prostrate themselves without complaint 'seven times on the belly and seven times on the back'. The very fact
that Tuthmosis III undertook annual expeditions shows that even he, with
his wealth and manpower, could not hope to dominate the area except through
a system of tributary princes who were nonetheless proud enough, and
spirited enough, to make trouble when they did not feel threatened. Although,
like his grandfather, he saw himself ruling from the Sudan to the Euphrates,
he would not have thought of cultural domination. He would not expect Amon

Previous page : Tuthmosis III wearing the royal nems, *or headdress, with
the insignia of royalty, the* uraeus *serpent*
*Opposite : The 'botanical garden' of Tuthmosis III, site of the carvings
of plants and animals brought back from Syria*

Above : The goddess Ma'at wearing the ostrich feather of truth in her hair and carrying two ankhs, *the symbols of eternal life*
Opposite : A statue of Sakhmet, the lion-headed goddess of war and destruction, in a temple dating from the time of Tuthmosis III

to be worshipped by Asiatics. He would not even have expected that Egyptian should be the international language of diplomacy. That was, and remained, Akkadian, a Mesopotamian language. The Egyptians had no ideology for export so they lived in Egypt and just camped in Retenu.

It was just that bit too early to expect an ideology with international application. For the most part men, even in the relatively advanced area of the fertile crescent from Mesopotamia through Syria and down to the Nile valley, were still too conscious of being part of great natural forces and having to struggle to keep their end up. Starvation, disease, and disasters such as earthquakes were not thought of in any impersonal way but as the will of some hostile spirit whom one could only seek to propitiate. This attitude is what lies behind all sacrifice. There was a readiness in Egypt to accept the idea of a totalitarian, god-directed state as a means of organizing this propitiation on the most effective scale. All the formalities, all the ritual, all the theology were rationalizations of propitiation in the hope that, to some limited degree, men could control their fate. Each people had a different view of what was required to achieve this control and therefore gods differed, and their rite differed, depending on where they lived. The circumstances of the Nile valley were unique and it would have been surprising if Egypt had been the birthplace of a universal religion; it certainly could not have been any development of the cult of Amon.

What characterized Egypt was the need for order. Egyptian religious beliefs had no great ethical content but in practical matters there was a general recognition that justice was a good so fundamental that it was part of the natural order of things. Pharaoh's adjuration to the Vizier on his appointment made that much clear; the word used, *Ma'at*, signified something more comprehensive than fairness. Originally the word was a physical term; it meant level, ordered, and symmetrical like the foundation plan of a temple. Later it came to mean righteousness, truth, and justice. Shakespeare can have known nothing about the values of ancient Egypt but the words, in *Troilus and Cressida*, he puts into the mouth of Ulysses, that justice depends on social harmony brought about by 'degree, priority and place' which the physical universe – the planets and the earth – observed, would have been regarded by Tuthmosis as correct but platitudinous. As a god himself he would have known that truth and justice extended throughout the universe; they could be seen in the regular procession of the circumpolar stars, the heliacal rising of the dog-star Sirius that marked the beginning of the year, the daily passage of the sun-god from dawn to dusk, and the annual flooding by the Nile. In spite of all the ills that flesh is heir to, the created world was good, its character was order with justice, its name was *Ma'at*, and it was personified by a spritely goddess with a feather in her hair.

Ma'at was a way of thinking about Egypt. She could have been exported only with difficulty and certainly not made the basis for any allegiance that transcended differences of language and tradition. Osiris, who died and rose again, might have had this universal appeal but Osiris was not a god in whose name one conquered; his time had yet to come and then only under a different name and with a richness of moral references that, in Christianity, made him unrecognizable. But in Bronze Age Egypt the goddess *Ma'at* was a reality for the most lowly peasant who, treated in a way that outraged his sense of natural justice, did not hesitate to appeal to her. The Vizier was the 'Scribe of *Ma'at*'. Because she held the people together under his godship pharaoh himself was a devotee. Tuthmosis, in sparing his defeated enemies at Megiddo, may have been motivated by a precise political calculation, but it is also possible he was animated by mercy which he had learned not from Amon but from his own sense of what men owed to one another in a cosmic order that was divinely ordained. As a god himself he had the appropriate status for making decisions of this kind.

It was not so easy at this time for the king to be accepted as a god as it had been earlier when, for most of his subjects, he was a remote and mysterious figure. Now the king was a warrior who, in battle, might owe his life to an ordinary man. He could be seen at close quarters and under stress. The god-king like Tuthmosis III had no alternative to being a hero whose deeds ordinary men might seek in vain to emulate. This was the heroic age of Egypt just as, so very shortly afterwards, the siege of Troy marked the heroic age of Greece. The Egyptian god simply had to show off in public and it would have been hard on the king who lacked the necessary skills. One favourite activity was to be driven very fast in a chariot past a number of targets which the king would try to hit with his arrows. Tuthmosis III liked to shoot at a thick plate of copper set up on a pole. With the whole army watching he drove an arrow from his composite bow into this target with such force that the head protruded from the other side. He was so delighted he had the copper plate with the arrow still in it set up in the temple so that Amon himself might see what the king was capable of. He was, too, a hunter of lions, the rhinoceros (a rarity this, on a Nubian campaign), and the elephant. He pursued wild cattle in his chariot. He loved wrestling and single-stick fencing. The king might be a god but he was, as never before, in the public eye. Queen Hatshepsut had never exhibited herself in this way.

Nearly every spring and summer Tuthmosis policed his vassal states in the north, sometimes fighting battles or conducting sieges, but often it was enough merely to make his presence known. His long-term objectives were to seize Kadesh, the rich fortress city of Tunip which was about thirty miles to the north, and to emulate his grandfather's achievement of crossing the Euphrates and invading the land of Mitanni. He was impressed by the part sea-power could play in land campaigning and put in hand a considerable expansion of the Egyptian navy. The dockyard was not, as might be expected, on the coast or even at Avaris on the Pelusiac branch of the Nile but at Perunefer near Memphis. Large numbers of broad-bottomed troop-ships were built of imported pine, birch, cedar, and the local acacia and sycamore. These Mediterranean boats were more robust than Nile craft and less speedy than the longer boats built for the Punt trade down the Red Sea. Each had a great overhead truss (a hogging truss) binding the front of the ship to the stern to prevent the ship 'hogging' on the crest of a wave and breaking its back. Unlike normal Egyptian craft they had keels, a foreign device for which imported Syrian workmen were probably responsible. It is evidence of the Egyptians' cultural tolerance that the Syrian deities Baal and Astarte were not only worshipped in Perunefer by the immigrant craftsmen but the new cults even gained adherents among the native population.

Tuthmosis' aim was to avoid the long march up through Palestine and Syria by transporting his army by sea. We do not know how many soldiers could be packed into these craft; if a hundred then the whole armada transporting four divisions of five thousand men each could scarcely have been less than two hundred ships. Stowage space for chariots and stalls for horses had to be provided. Each ship had a large, rectangular, loose-footed sail – that is, without a lower yard as in older Nile boats; rolling in the sea might cause a fixed yard to dip in the water and capsize the boat. Even if the guess that Tuthmosis sailed out with two hundred ships is an exaggeration and some of the force, the chariotry for example, went by land, the armada must nevertheless have been large and its building a major industrial achievement.

Early in the year the unsettled weather that brought rain to the northern Delta could also bring winds from the south-west favourable to the Syrian voyage; but the prevailing winds are from the north making for an easier and quicker return. Navigation depended very much on oarsmen, twenty-two or thirty-four to a vessel, naked but for a net loincloth with a leather seat. It was normal practice to hug the shore ready to put into harbour or run the ships up on the beach at the first sign of bad weather. The sails being very broad in relation to their height and brightly patterned in squares and circles of red, white, and yellow, the fleet would, seen from some headland in Retenu, have looked like a cloud of butterflies on the blue water. The ships were business-like craft but they were not without the appropriate embellishments. At the prow of each would be a carved lion's head with a Syrian's head in its mouth. Forward and aft were representations of Montu. Watch was kept from a crow's nest at the top of the mast; this was even more important on the return than on the outward voyage because the desired Egyptian landfall was notoriously difficult to make on that low-lying coast with a strong west to east current running along it. In exceptionally good conditions the voyage from Byblos might have been completed in less than a week.

In charge of the dockyard at Perunefer (which means 'Good departure' or 'Bon voyage') was no less a person than the Crown Prince Amenophis him-

Amenophis II shooting at a target, from a temple at Karnak

self, son of Tuthmosis III by his Chief Wife Meryetre-Hatshepsut, a big, tough, and perhaps brutal young man who was a great exponent of the hunting, shooting, and athletic tradition that was growing up among the leading families. Horses were his passion. He studied them, trained them in person, and liked nothing better than to be out on the hard desert sand in his chariot with them. 'They would never grow tired when he took the reins, nor would they sweat even at a gallop.' As an archer he was supreme. Like Odysseus he had a bow no other man could draw and he soon took up his father's game of riding in a chariot at full speed to shoot arrows through copper targets three inches thick – so it was claimed. Tuthmosis's pride in such a youth can be understood. He was the ideal divisional commander under his father's generalship, leading his troops into rich Syrian cities where they plundered, glutted themselves, anointed themselves with oil daily, and got drunk 'as if at a festival in Egypt'.

By 1465 BC Tuthmosis was in control of Palestine, the Damascus area, and the coast of Lebanon and Syria sufficiently far north for him to use the ports as supply bases from which he could launch attacks into the Orontes valley and across to Mitanni or, as it was increasingly called, Naharin beyond the Euphrates. The Mitannians are still a somewhat obscure people. Their capital, Washshukani has never been found, though it must have been somewhere in the bulge between the upper Tigris and Euphrates. Their ancestors were Hurrians whose homeland was present-day Armenia. They spoke a distinctive language, unrelated to the Semitic languages found further east and south; nor was it an Indo-European language like that of the Hittites to the north and west. The Hurrians moved down, it seems, into Upper Mesopotamia up to a thousand years before the Egyptians appeared on the scene, by which time a further wave of Indo-European pastoralists who bred horses and fought from chariots moved in. They were fighting people who established themselves as an aristocracy in Hurrian lands, in the course of time came to speak Hurrian themselves, and presided over a loosely structured empire that stretched across much of modern northern Iraq and northern Syria to the Mediterranean. Cities in Syria like Kadesh and Tunip had Hurrian populations and *maryanna* overlords, and the strong resistance they put up to Egyptian aggression was no doubt encouraged and assisted by their kin across the Euphrates. Hence Tuthmosis' determination to strike at what he would naturally regard as the heartland of his enemies. But how could he transport an army quickly and efficiently across the Euphrates? His grandfather had taken not much more than a division over and they did not stay long. Tuthmosis had greater ambitions.

He had a small armada of boats built in the land of Megau, which was either on the Mediterranean coast of Syria or on the Orontes, and transported overland in sections by ox-cart. This technique of shipbuilding in parts that could be dismantled and then reassembled may well have been devised by the Egyptians for their Red Sea trade with Punt. The fast Punt boats could have been built in parts at Coptos on the Nile and trundled through the Wadi Hammamat to the sea at Qoseir where they were put together again and launched. (Some of the sea anchors, blocks of stone with holes through them, are there to this day.) The Egyptians were experienced naval architects and it is no longer supposed, as once used to be the case, that they acquired all their skills in the making of seafaring boats from the Syrians or Cretans.

From the Orontes to Carchemish on the Euphrates is a hundred miles in a straight line but this is difficult hill country and the journey would have been very much longer by ox-waggon. The ships went in advance of the main body of troops, no doubt with a strong guard, but even so it is hard to understand why the king of Mitanni did not pounce on them. A bad intelligence service no doubt had something to do with it. But one has the impression, too, that Mitanni did not put really substantial forces into the field on this campaign, rather as though they had decided to adopt guerilla tactics and draw Tuthmosis further and further from his base.

The first time Tuthmosis encountered Mitannian troops was in a small-scale engagement near Aleppo. He brushed them aside. When he did arrive south of Carchemish, assemble his boats, and cross the Euphrates, of the enemy in force there was no sign. He set up a celebratory stela to accompany the one set up by his grandfather sixty years before and then marched south, in evident impatience at not being able to get to grips with the enemy, setting fire to villages from which the populations had mostly fled. Undoubtedly the

Egyptians were in such strength that the king of Mitanni wanted to avoid a pitched battle. The Egyptian line of communication was extended and he was content to wait for the invaders to retire across the river, which they did just where the Euphrates makes a great bend to the east before flowing down to Babylon.

This was Tuthmosis' eighth campaign and he still had many more before him. Whether he realized it or not at the time this raid across the Euphrates – for whatever his intentions this is all it was – marked the geographical limits of his achievements. Truth to tell, although it had been an impressive demonstration of his power, the adventure did not bring the direct results he had looked for – only a miserable three prisoners taken, thirty women and six hundred or so slaves. He did, however, make indirect gains. In the eyes of the other great powers in the area, the Hittites, the Assyrians from their base further east on the Tigris, and the Babylonians, Tuthmosis had made a substantial point at the expense of Mitanni – welcome from their point of view – and they sent presents and congratulations. Among the presents was a crate containing four domestic fowls 'that lay eggs every day'. To the Egyptians this was a marvel.

What was remarkable about Tuthmosis' operations in Asia was the logistical skill with which they were carried out. No detail was too small to escape his consideration, from supplies the Mediterranean ports must have in their warehouses so that his army was properly victualled to considerations of how he could move that army from one place to another with greater speed. No other people of the time had the Egyptian capacity for organizing large numbers of men in some concerted activity, whether it was transporting obelisks from Aswan to Thebes or simply controlling them on the battlefield with a system of trumpet calls. What evidently counted more than meticulous planning by Tuthmosis' chiefs of staff and quartermasters-general was his own determination. Every soldier in the army felt that Tuthmosis knew precisely what he was up to at all times. Tuthmosis wanted the vassal princes to be in just that frame of mind too.

He thought of the years to come. As part of his plan for the permanent Egyptian domination of Palestine and Syria Tuthmosis did his best to ensure that the vassal princes were Egyptianized. The policy of carrying off young *maryanna* and educating them in Egypt was Tuthmosis' own idea. 'The children of the chiefs and their brothers were brought back to Egypt and placed in strongholds. Now, whenever a chief died in Retenu His Majesty would cause his son to stand in his place.' It would be interesting to know what this indoctrination consisted of; the ability to read and write Egyptian, perhaps, though there is no evidence for this and indeed quite a lot to show that Asian princes, including those of client states, never wrote to pharaoh except in their own different languages. The hostages would be told something of Egypt's past but they would not have been subjected to any religious proselytization. The aim would be to impress the might and majesty of Egypt on these young foreigners so that they would hesitate to make trouble once back in their own countries. The mention of strongholds implies that whatever they learned of Egypt was mainly from their guards and the scribes who were under instruction to visit them.

We know so much about the campaigns of Tuthmosis III because of the lengthy and detailed accounts of them given on the walls of the Hall of Annals which enclosed the sanctuary of Amon at Karnak. A personal and, perhaps, not very accurate supplement to the official record can be found inscribed on the walls of a Theban tomb, that of the soldier Amenemhab who served under Tuthmosis and later his son Amenophis II. Amenemhab reports his personal successes; so many prisoners taken, so many donkeys, so many spears. The king would award prisoners as personal slaves to soldiers who had distinguished themselves. When really large numbers of prisoners were taken they would not be disposed of in this way but marched back to Egypt, accompanied by women and children, to be handed over to the great temples for work on their increasingly large estates. Hands were struck from the dead and counted before the king to establish the number of enemy killed in any particular battle.

After every skirmish, battle or siege brought to a successful conclusion the army scribes would go meticulously to work recording the booty on leather scrolls. From his travelling treasure chests Tuthmosis would cause to be produced gold necklaces, bracelets, rings, lions, and flies (the Gold of Honour), and award them as medals are awarded nowadays. Grandeur travelled with him, even on campaigns, so although he might sit in a tent of an evening it would be on a gold-panelled throne placed on a dais so that he was on a higher level than his officers. With the flaps rolled up on two sides to admit the cooler evening air he would want detailed reports on the events of the day. Tribute received and booty taken, whether in humans or treasure, would be of particular interest to him; the details would in due course be presented to Amon who was now getting so rich that he may have started to finance campaigns with a view to a profitable return, rather as some city merchant would finance a voyage in Elizabethan times. Tuthmosis would be thinking not only of this campaign but of the next one too, and the one after that. As he looked out across some Syrian valley, noisy with cascades, while the smell of roast duck floated up from the field kitchens, he would be busy with calculations. These mountain forests were under the protection of a local goddess, the Lady of Byblos. How could it be contrived that she accepted that all cedar was an Egyptian monopoly? Such an understanding was desirable but how could it be enforced? Perhaps he was relying too much on controlling the land by his annual prowl and what he really ought to be planning was a string of impregnable fortresses like the one he had already established south of Beruta.

Once a precedent had been established in Egypt it was usually followed.

Asian plants in the 'botanical garden' of Tuthmosis III at Karnak

In going to the Euphrates at all Tuthmosis had imitated his grandfather. In smaller things, too, he imitated him by going on an elephant hunt in the marshes of the Orontes. A hundred and twenty of the animals had been sighted. The opportunity for securing so much ivory was not to be missed and, as Amenemhab tells the story, the king himself was in danger from the largest of the herd. Amenemhab distracted the wounded animal in some way and took refuge in the water where he stood between two rocks. There is no word for an elephant's trunk in Egyptian so all Amenemhab could then claim was that he cut off its hand. To anyone who knows the country it is extraordinary that herds of elephants were to be found there as recently as the time of the pharaohs. The climate must have been wetter to supply the vegetation they depended on for food. They were smaller than modern elephants but they still needed a lot to eat.

What the story does remind us of is the deserted nature of these parts. Between the fortified cities and the fields that fed them were vast, empty areas of scrub and desert where the only humans were nomadic tribesmen who moved about in search of grazing. In lusher parts there was space for elephants to roam. Tuthmosis himself was so impressed by the unfamiliar plants and flowers he saw that he made a collection of them and when he came to build his great Festival Hall at Karnak had them represented, not very accurately it must be admitted, together with birds and animals on its walls. He was characteristically Egyptian in the delight he took in animals and flowers.

Kadesh remained a problem. Durusha, the ruler of the city, still flourishing long after his humiliation at Megiddo, was the most adroit of Tuthmosis' enemies. He never accepted a state of vassalage or came to terms. In spite of breaching the walls of his city and capturing the place, Tuthmosis had to come back and do the same thing all over again. He was still fighting Durusha on his very last Syrian campaign, in the forty-second year of his reign when, to distract the stallions of the Egyptian chariotry, the prince released a mare in front of them. Just as he had dealt with the elephant so Amenemhab now handled the threat presented by the mare. He pursued the mare on foot, killed her by ripping open her belly with his sword, and then presented the tail to the king. Amenemhab was the first through the breach in the wall ('I was the one who pierced it, being the first of all the valiant; no other before me did it.') but there is no mention of Durusha who presumably escaped as he had escaped before and taken refuge on the other side of the Euphrates.

Even for Tuthmosis Syria was always dangerous country, mainly because of Mitannian infiltration, that could only be ventured into in force. He was so secure in Palestine, though, that Intef his herald would precede him to commandeer palaces, see that they were purified, furnished, and stocked with food and wine. His progress would be a royal one, receiving tribute of gold, silver, oil, incense, and wine, which would all be recorded by Intef. Time off would be taken for hunting. But enough was enough and for the remaining twelve years of his reign Tuthmosis did not go personally into Asia though the machinery of control by commissars continued to function with as much efficiency as though he did. Presents and tribute continued to flow in. The tomb of the Vizier Rekhmire has scenes showing the offering of tribute from all parts of the known world. The use of the word 'tribute' can be misleading; it was used to describe all valuable imports, whether by way of offerings from vassals in Retenu or by way of trade with the inhabitants of countries the Egyptians never controlled, like Crete or Punt.

International trade was largely a royal prerogative based on barter in which the value of goods was, however, related to given weights of gold, silver, and copper. There was an elaborate bureaucracy to deal with this trade. Since the quantity and value of the goods imported demonstrated the power and majesty of the king, the scribes did not bother to distinguish between gifts and what was purchased. In Rekhmire's tomb men from Punt are shown presenting balsam plants, ostrich feathers, a live baboon, a cheetah, and gum in the perhaps surprisingly Egyptian form of miniature pyramids or obelisks. There does seem to have been an ancient cultural and racial link between

Egypt and Punt. Both peoples were Hamitic and some princes of Punt even wore the royal beard. Are there pyramids to be discovered in Somalia? From Crete and the islands, fair-skinned men in unusually patterned kilts present vases, bullion, jewellery, and daggers. Black Nubians bring gold ingots in bars and rings, a green monkey, and hunting dogs. From Syria come captives – men, women, and children all destined for a life of slavery. One reason for the flow of such commerce was that it was based on the purchasing power of gold and copper; and Egypt had more gold than any other country.

By this time, most Egyptian kings celebrated the Tail Festival, or *Heb-Sed*, on the thirtieth anniversary of his coronation, though some kings not expecting to last so long or out of impatience are known to have celebrated it earlier. A king who ruled an exceptionally long time, like Ramesses II, had festivals not only on the thirtieth anniversary but at comparatively short intervals, perhaps three years, after. Just what went on at a *Sed* festival and what its significance was are uncertain but not beyond all conjecture. It was clearly intended to renew the king's vitality and to re-enact the unification of Upper and Lower Egypt. Its name comes from the animal's tail – usually a bull's – which formed part of the king's insignia.

Tuthmosis III celebrated his first *Sed* festival in the normal way, on the thirtieth anniversary of his accession (which dated from the death of Tuthmosis II and ignored the Hatshepsut reign), probably at Memphis, which was the traditional site. The figure of Osiris was enthroned in a specially built pavilion and played an important but obscure part in the ceremonies. From this it has been supposed that this ancient festival, which dated back to the actual unification of the country in 3200 BC, had even more ancient elements in it, of the ritual sacrifice of the king whose blood was needed to renew the fertility of the land. If so, Tuthmosis III was probably unaware of it. So far as he was concerned it was a reaffirmation of his kingship over the two lands and a receiving of homage. The rejoicings lasted several days and there was a great consumption of beer and food.

He held court in a specially built festival pavilion. Wearing a short pleated cloak he would formally be crowned again with the White Crown of the south which was a tall conical linen hat with bulbous top, and the Red Crown of the north which was low and cylindrical, made of reeds, with a high peak at the back and a curlicue at the front. He ran a double course round a marked field to symbolize his encompassing the two lands, took part in a ritual dance, and, in the sanctuaries of Horus and Seth, was presented with four arrows by the gods themselves – or, rather, priests wearing Horus and Seth masks. Tuthmosis directed these arrows to the four cardinal points of the compass in a magic assault on all possible enemies. In a long line of booths opposite the canopied dais on which the throne was placed were the images of all the gods of Egypt with their attendant priests – Hathor, the cow-goddess of Dendera, the ram-headed god Khnum from Elephantine who had fashioned man on a potter's wheel, Nekhebet the vulture-goddess from El-Kab, and all the others in the form of men, women, birds, or animals – the crocodile, dog, scorpion, cobra, baboon, hippopotamus, the whole range of sacred animals with which the gods were associated. The king 'poured water' for each and all.

To mark the occasion Tuthmosis had seven obelisks erected, five in Thebes and two in Heliopolis, none of which is now standing on its original site. (Cleopatra's Needle on the Victoria Embankment in London and the obelisk in Central Park, New York, are the two from Heliopolis.) As an impressive adjunct to the Temple of Amon at Karnak he built a Festival Hall in stone with unusual features; the central columns of this hall are in the shape of tent-poles, inversely tapering so that they are thickest at the top, very like the wooden poles that supported his great pavilion at Memphis for the *Sed* festival. Either he wanted the great occasion perpetuated in this way or the Hall itself was used for his second *Heb-Sed* in year 33 of his reign.

Although Tuthmosis no longer went campaigning in Asia he made expeditions into Nubia right up to the last. The Nile flows from south to north but there is one section in Nubia where the course exceptionally is north-east to south-west. In the middle of this stretch is the Fourth Cataract, about seven hundred miles of river-travel south of Thebes, and near here is an isolated outcrop of rock known as Gebel Barkal. This is the 'sacred mountain' which overlooks the fortified town of Napata already established by the time of Tuthmosis III. Like the much earlier Buhen it was a high-walled, rectangular, mud-brick fortification with bastions, towers, and a great gateway, standing among barley fields and groves of dom and date palm. This was the southern limit of permanent Egyptian administration; Nehi, the highly efficient Viceroy of Tuthmosis, divided his time between it and Buhen which was the main administrative centre. The navigation of the Fourth Cataract is particularly difficult and this must have deterred Tuthmosis from trying to establish a base above it, near the modern village of Abu Hamed, for example, which was at the southern end of the caravan route from Elephantine which cut off the great western bend of the Nile.

Something like ten thousand ounces, troy weight, of gold went back every year to Tuthmosis from the desert valleys north of this point, between the Nile and the Red Sea. It was won by laboriously crushing to powder quartz with traces of gold in it and then washing the powder in stone troughs so that the heavier gold was sorted out. Conditions were extremely harsh for the gangs, made up in the main of prisoners and criminals, who did this work. In summer the heat was intolerable even for Egyptians and there was a permanent shortage of drinking water. At the entrance to each valley was a military post where the mineral gold was fused into ingots before onward transmission to Egypt. What military activity there was now mainly consisted of dealing with the tribesmen when they tried to interfere with the gold mining. They

The weighing of ingots from the tomb of Rekhmire who served Tuthmosis III and Amenophis II as vizier

often lived in caves, so the usual procedure would be to locate the caves, destroy the few wretched possessions the troglodytes had, drive off their cattle, and, if possible, take prisoners and carry them off to slavery in Egypt. This was normally the job of the Vizier but Tuthmosis himself made at least one expedition into the most southerly part of his empire. The old canal at the First Cataract originally made by King Senusret III and cleared by Tuthmosis I now had to be cleared again for the passage of his grandson and this time he characteristically gave the fishermen of Elephantine instructions to maintain the canal in perpetuity.

To set up a stela, as Tuthmosis did, on the 'sacred mountain' at Gebel Barkal recording his Syrian campaigns was to make a statement about empire at a point where he plainly thought it important to make that statement. 'Vile Kush', he was saying, consider what has happened at the other end of the world and tremble. It did not matter that the tribesmen of Kush would be unable to read what the stela said about his northerly exploits against 'the wretched man' of Kadesh and 'those whom god held in horror', the Mitannians. The communication was magic. Back at Thebes the king would be able to think with satisfaction of the two stelae, one beyond the Euphrates in Naharin and the other deep in black Africa, proclaiming like surrogate heralds his majesty at the limits of empire. For him, what was represented or written down was no mere picture or set of words; it was alive, as he was alive, and the barbarians would not dare to touch his stelae, any more than they would dare to touch him.

Important though these remote stelae might be it was even more important to ensure that the record was preserved at Thebes. In addition to the campaign annals inscribed on the corridor walls round the sanctuary at Karnak, Tuthmosis had a black granite tablet about six feet tall engraved with what has been described as his Hymn of Victory. The hand of the king himself has been detected in its composition. If indeed he played some part in it he has not followed the usual practice of addressing Amon-Re but he has adopted the dramatic device of causing the god himself to speak. This implies immense confidence. In the course of twenty-five lines most of the peoples of the known world are named: Mitanni, Nubians, Hittites, Beduin nomads, Libyans, Cypriots, Cretans, and Hellenes. Whether Tuthmosis had actually fought with them or not – and there is no evidence of war with Crete or the Islands of the Sea – they are represented as tyrannized by him. He appears in forms most likely to dismay them – a crocodile on the Euphrates, a burning sun in Lebanon, a fiery comet in Arabia, a lion god, a young bull. The Hymn has such a geographical sweep that it set the pattern for much of the later royal rhetoric on temple walls.

But to say 'Tuthmosis caused the god to speak' is to describe what happened in a way the king and the Chief Priest would not have accepted. The modern no-nonsense view of Amon-Re is that he was a puppet manipulated by the real possessors of power, the king and the Chief Priest, and it might further be suggested that this manipulation was conducted with a certain amount of cynicism. It would be wrong to pretend we can disentangle the threads of calculated expediency and religious veneration that made up Tuthmosis's attitude to 'his father'. Analytical reasoning was not a characteristic of the Egyptians and they would not have known how to separate the religious from the secular. Thoughts and actions we might attribute to the king or a priest might by him be attributed to an inspiration from the god; he could communicate only through human agency – or through pharaoh, who was both a being of flesh and blood and yet 'the good god' – but that did not mean trickery. Even though the statue of the god could be manipulated by strings, could move its head and arms, could even, perhaps, place the crown on the king's head at his coronation, and could speak through the mouth of a priest, the underlying conviction would be that the acts and words were of divine origin. How contradictions were resolved we do not know. The most striking one was the statement made by Amon-Re at one time that Hatshepsut possessed his soul and that she was to 'exercise the excellent kingship in the whole land' while at another time he picked out Tuthmosis III for the king-ship. Tuthmosis must have seen the reliefs at Deir el-Bahri showing Hatshep-sut's conception – scenes that affronted him. In ordering the removal of her name he would have seen himself as under instruction by Amon to remove a lie for which Hatshepsut and not Amon had been responsible. All that could be said with confidence was that decision making by Amon was a subtle and complex process in which there might be errors of interpretation by such as Hatshepsut which subsequent pharaohs would have to set right. That is how Tuthmosis would have seen it. In contrast with Hatshepsut's propaganda Tuthmosis' Hymn of Victory would be considered, by him, a communica-tion from the god of unquestioned authenticity. Witness the manner in which it had been given.

An utterance of the god such as this Hymn was not set down on papyrus and then just handed to artists so that it could be set up in relief hieroglyphs on a tablet. It would first have to be heard from the god himself, in the course no doubt of some long and complicated temple service. There is no record of an utterance being made in this way but it would accord with everything we know of the behaviour expected of Amon at this time; someone who be-haved very like a human being and could be asked to intervene directly in affairs of state. His boat shrine was so large and weighty it took twenty-six priests to bear it on poles into the pillared hall where the king stood on the dais before his throne. Tuthmosis knew, and everyone else in that gathering of the great knew, that this was the supreme public act of approval by the god for the king's imperial achievements. Amon-Re had sailed into the presence of this great congregation and was actually there in the cabin of his boat as witness of his divine love for the king.

To be in the great temple everyone present had been purified and was in the ancient equivalent of a state of grace. The King's Great Wife, God's Wife of Amon, Meryetre-Hatshepsut, stood at the head of the women musicians and singers known as the Concubines of the God. The Crown Prince Amenophis was at his father's right hand. The Chief Priest, the various other categories of priests and prophets down to the ordinary priests (who served one month on and three months off, rather like the watches kept on a ship), the Viceroy of Nubia better known as the King's Son of Kush, the Vizier for Upper Egypt, the Vizier for Lower Egypt, the mayor of Thebes, and other great dignitaries and their retainers all stood in the aromatic, incense-impregnated dimness. The early morning light came from high clerestory windows and there was a multitude of flickering oil lamps.

Led by the queen herself the priestesses of the temple recognized the presence of the god with the jangling of metal rattles, the *sistra*. Menkheper-rasonb, the Chief Priest, with shaven head and in a simple tunic of white linen, intoned the recognized greeting, which was 'Amon-Re, Lord of Karnak, is raised up on the high seat', and from the ranks of priests and prophets behind him came a response: 'Your beauties are your own, O Amon-Re, Lord of Karnak.' Or some such ritual.

The effect of the dim light, the incense, the tinkling of the *sistra*, and the heat would be to create an atmosphere in which almost anything could be believed to happen. If a priest stood before the shrine and intoned the words that follow, who was there to question that the god himself was speaking?

> Utterance of Amon-Re, Lord of Thebes,
> Thou comest to me, thou exultest, seeing my beauty,
> O my son, my avenger, Menkheperre, living forever.

Menkheperre was another of the names of Tuthmosis III, his throne name, the one he took when he became king. As he listened to the god's recital of his achievements ('Thou hast crossed the water of the Great Bend of Naharin' – crossed the Euphrates into the land of Mitanni, that is to say) he might well have thought that his ascendancy had been established for ever. ('Thou hast made captive the princes of Retenu. . . . The lands of Mitanni tremble in fear of thee. . . . I have come, causing thee to smite the Nubian troglodytes. . . . Thy monuments are greater than any king who has been.') Never before had an Egyptian king enjoyed such a sense of international power. Surrounded by so much pomp and adulation it was blindingly clear to Tuthmosis that what Amon-Re had given, no other god or man could take away.

5
THE GOLDEN
MERIDIAN

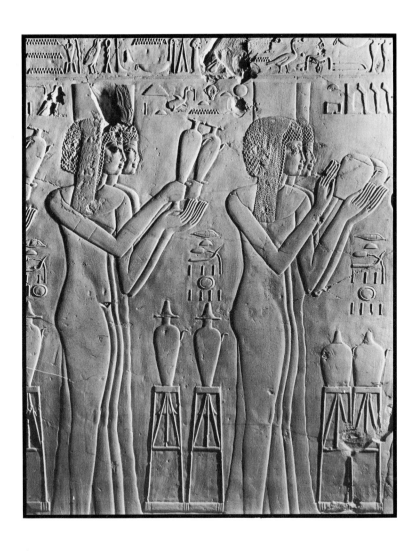

IN THE BOOK OF GENESIS WE ARE TOLD
that Joseph married the daughter of a priest of On. Almost nothing of the
ancient city now survives, only part of the outer wall that enclosed the temple
and an obelisk set up by Senusret I who ruled more than four hundred years
before Tuthmosis III, but if more remains from his time had survived they
would show Tuthmosis ascribing his great achievements not to Amon, back
home in Thebes, but to the sun-god. For this is the place the Greeks called
Heliopolis, the City of the Sun. In the various names and guises with which
the sun-god manifested himself he had been worshipped here from the most
ancient times: Atum ('the Accomplished One'), Harakhte ('Horus of the
Horizon'), Khepri ('the one who has come into being', alias 'the Scarab'),
Harmachis ('Horus in the Horizon', alias 'the Great Sphinx at Gizeh') or Re,
the sun-god himself who was represented as a hawk-headed man with a sun
disc on his head.

Even at the time of Amon's ascendancy Heliopolis was a great religious
centre. In scholarship and theology there was no other centre in Egypt to
rival it. Egyptian kings came here to be crowned – Hatshepsut, that great
devotee of Amon, among them. Re was so ancient and revered that when the
Theban kings ousted the Hyksos and assumed power throughout Egypt,
Amon himself, their local god, was transformed into a god acceptable throughout the Two Lands by saying he was not just a god of procreation or of the
wind and air but he was a sun-god too. He was not just Amon. He was Amon-
Re. But the sun cult at Heliopolis remained, and was observed just as though
Amon-Re did not exist. In the eyes of the priesthood of Heliopolis theirs was
the orthodox religion. All others were variants. On an obelisk Tuthmosis III
set up in Heliopolis (now in Central Park, New York), he made no reference
to Amon-Re. His victories, he said, had been made possible by the sun-god
Re and no other. 'His father Re has decreed for him victory against every
land, and might of the sword by his arms, in order to widen the boundaries
of Egypt.'

The fact is that the Egyptians were so conservative they could take on new
gods without discarding the old. They did not worry about contradictions or

*Previous page : The daughters of Amenophis III carrying vases on the
occasion of the Sed festival which marked the thirtieth anniversary of his
accession. From a frieze in the tomb of Kheraef*

inconsistencies. The very ancient religious beliefs and practices that centred on the murdered Osiris and his resurrection were quite separate from any sky religion. It was possible for a scribe of Thebes, say, to acknowledge Amon as a helper in time of need, pray to the sun-god Re-Harakhte for favours, and arrange for his mummy to make the river journey to Abydos, the centre of the Osiris cult, for a ceremony that gave assurance of life after death. In this undogmatic world even the architects of Amon's temple could write hymns to the sun-god. 'Sole lord,' says the stela of the twin brothers Suty and Hor, 'who taketh captive all lands every day.' There is another stela between the paws of the Great Sphinx ascribed to the grandson of Tuthmosis III which records that the young man – he became Tuthmosis IV – was promised the throne on condition he removed the sand which half-buried the Sphinx who said he was the sun-god, Harmachis-Khepri-Atum. This same Tuthmosis IV ascribed on a scarab his victories to the sun-god who is here for the first time called Aten. Previously this word had meant quite simply 'solar disc'. Now it meant something more. So even at the time of Amon's greatest power the ancient sun religion of Egypt was alive and flourishing.

Tuthmosis III died in 1436 BC after a reign of fifty-four years and thereafter the sun religion seemed, if anything, to be regaining any ground it may have lost. It is tempting to see the emphasis placed on it as an intended curb on the power of the priests of Amon. Other cults flourished too. Amenophis II, who succeeded his father, was at one time Chief Priest of Ptah at Memphis. The whole country had been so transformed by its military successes and so much wealth had flowed in that the priests of Heliopolis and Memphis may not have cast envious eyes at the disproportionate amount of it going to Amon; their own foundations flourished too, if more modestly. What was of greater importance for the future than any rivalry between priests of different cults was the fact that they now formed part of a professional corps that had an increasing control of temple wealth. Since this came to be such a big part of national wealth the priestly caste potentially constituted a state within a state. Everything depended on the vigour and ability of the pharaoh. Tuthmosis III ruled his priests with the same firmness that he ruled the army. But an indolent pharaoh and an energetic Chief Priest of Amon-Re would create uncertainties about where power in the state actually lay.

Of this there is no evidence during the reign of Amenophis II because he was a strong personality who used the powers of the pharaoh to the full. In contrast to his father's more conciliatory approach to relations with foreign princes, Amenophis plainly despised them and was merciless when there was disaffection. Following such a father as his he had a great deal to live up to. He compensated for what he lacked in shrewdness by what he would have regarded as greater vigour. All these Syrians understood was the sword! He really did club prisoners to death before the shrine of Amon. He had six of the corpses hung up on the enclosure wall at Thebes and a seventh sent south to be displayed on the wall of Napata as a warning to Kush that His Majesty would put up with no nonsense.

If the official reports of his two Asiatic campaigns, as inscribed on stelae, are to be believed, Amenophis was a rash commander who occasionally pressed on alone only to find himself in the presence of the enemy whom he then proceeded to destroy single-handed. In reality he was neither so rash nor quite the solo all-conquering warrior. He boasted of superhuman deeds because he wanted to be seen as a hero king who could out-fight armies single-handed, who could row six times as far as two hundred men without stopping, and could drink anyone under the table. In the course of a drinking bout he dashed off a letter to his Viceroy in Nubia which so impressed the recipient with its informal – and perhaps incoherent – references to foreign princes, one of whom was described as an old woman, and to the magicians of Nubia, that he had it set up on a stela. Amenophis II may have regretted this.

Impetuosity does seem to have been a weakness of military commanders at this time. Even Tuthmosis III had to be restrained. His son would rush along what he took to be the path of glory, only to find the rest of the army unable to keep up with him. On one occasion he had taken the vanguard across the Orontes, in spate from melted snows, only to turn and see the main army being engaged from the city of Katna; he was able, he claimed, to take them in surprise from the rear. Quite alone, except for personal servants, he would keep watch over the captured enemy and their baggage. One wonders what the rest of the army was doing. Amenophis mentions two ditches of fire enclosing the prisoners. The Egyptian troops were probably directed to cut brushwood and make a ring of bonfires that would serve two purposes, keep them warm during the cold Syrian night and provide enough illumination to prevent the Syrians from escaping unobserved.

From his two campaigns vast numbers of prisoners were brought back, including 270 female musicians with their instruments of gold and silver. There were Apiru prisoners too, wandering groups who had no fortified city to fall back on as the Syrians had. Large numbers of Canaanites were brought in. Amenophis' ruthlessness seems, on the face of it, to have achieved a long-lasting pacification of the area, because for the remaining seventeen or so years of his reign he did not need to go campaigning in Asia. But the calm may have been induced by a new balance of power in the north. Mitanni, the Kassite dynasty at Babylon, and the Hittites were in such uneasy relationship that any ambition one of them might have for Syrian adventures was curbed by fear of attack from the other two in alliance with Egypt.

The East was entering a period of peace and stability. Perhaps it would be

Tribute bearers from foreign lands shown in the tomb of Rekhmire : top are men from Punt ; in the centre Minoans bearing vases ; and at the bottom Nubians with a giraffe, ivory, and monkeys

truer to say that the period had started well back in the reign of Tuthmosis III and the two campaigns of Amenophis II had been provoked by the various princes of the area doing what they normally did when pharaoh died – test his successor with an attempt to get rid of Egyptian dominance. Trade flourished. Merchants set out from Babylon for some Mediterranean port – Ugarit was the greatest – where their lapis-lazuli and other goods could be shipped on to Egypt and bartered for papyrus, linen, and cereal grains. Laden donkeys trotted the caravan routes with leather goods, woollen cloth, and Syrian wine. Sea trading was dominated by Egyptian shipping, carrying timber from Lebanon, vases and ornaments from Crete, a new kind of humped cattle from somewhere in Upper Mesopotamia, copper, tin, silver, and even the mysterious amber which, after passing through many hands, had arrived from the remote north. Syrian merchants are known to have traded up the Nile and tethered their ships at the great quays of Thebes where they set up stalls – showing that a little trade, at least, could be carried on outside the state monopoly. Goods came from as far afield as Afghanistan, the Baltic, and equatorial Africa.

From Napata in the south to Hattushash in Anatolia, the Hittite capital, and to Washshukani of Naharin beyond the Euphrates in the north, couriers travelled with greetings, requests, gifts, warnings, news of the death of one king and the succession of another – a most important international courtesy this – and even the occasional loan of a wonder-working effigy. From the Egyptian point of view the most remarkable approach came from the old enemy, Mitanni, who sent a peace mission to Thebes towards the end of the reign of Amenophis II. An Egyptian scribe described this as an unparalleled event. Nothing like it had happened 'since the time of men and gods'. This eventually led to diplomatic marriages. Princesses from Mitanni were offered up on the altar of power politics, and were sent on the long, dusty journey to pharaoh's harem, the first being the daughter of the Mitannian King Arta-tama. She became the wife of Amenophis II's son Tuthmosis. It was the usual way of cementing an alliance. The Hittites recognized the political reality that such a marriage represented and became, as was intended, cautious.

After a period of domestic turmoil in Hatti, when there were more than the usual number of royal assassinations, the Hittite king who had reigned some twenty-five years or so before Tuthmosis III – his name was Telepinus – set up a new regime in which the succession to the throne was established by law and the military aristocracy of this Anatolian group of peoples had what they regarded as their ancient privileges restored. They built immense fortified cities of which Hattushash was the largest. From this power base this energetic people had made forays into Babylonia and Syria, and it was precisely to

Two scenes of tribute from Western Asia being presented

check this challenge that the Mitanni were eager to come to an understanding with Egypt. It was surprising the balance of power lasted as long as it did.

Edward Gibbon wrote that, 'If a man were called to fix the period in the history of the world during which the condition of the human race was most happy and prosperous, he would, without hesitation, name that which elapsed from the death of Domitian to the accession of Commodus.' The reign of the Antonines (AD 138–180) was 'possibly the only period of history in which the happiness of a great people was the sole object of government'. Gibbon knew little of the history of Ancient Egypt – the decipherment of Egyptian writing, which made the knowledge of such a history possible, was not achieved until some thirty years after his death. If he had enjoyed the benefit of modern knowledge of Ancient Egypt, it is doubtful whether he would have modified that well-known passage in *The Decline and Fall of the Roman Empire*. But if one had to choose a time in Ancient Egyptian history when life in the Nile valley was most genial and secure, it would, no doubt, be the golden years of the Egyptian empire, under Amenophis II, Tuthmosis IV, and, more especially, Amenophis III – the years from about 1450 to 1380 BC – when there was no major campaigning beyond the limits of Egypt, the wealth from the empire continued to flow in, the better-off classes enjoyed a standard of living their ancestors would not have dreamed of and their descendants looked back to with envy. Skilled craftsmen who had produced weapons of war turned to what we would call consumer goods. A family of workers who had once embellished chariots now produced striped glass fish for sale on the open market. A wide new range of luxury goods became available for the enriched office-holders of the all-powerful state.

In the later Roman Republic there is evidence of an almost limitless ambition to extend the Roman frontiers. The example of Alexander who had marched victoriously to India was always present in the minds of the senate and consuls, and it remained for Augustus to say there were certain geographical limits beyond which Rome, out of self-interest, should not seek to go. There is no evidence of any such decision being taken by Amenophis II, Tuthmosis IV, or even by the greatly more relaxed and luxurious Amenophis III but that, in effect, was what happened. Instead of fighting the Hittites and the Mitannians – still less the remoter Babylonians – the arts of exchanging gifts internationally now took over, their value calculated precisely to balance what was received.

These later pharaohs of the Theban dynasty are so different from their predecessors that foreign marriages – and one foreign marriage in particular –

Opposite above : Cargo-carrying river craft of the time of Amenophis III from the tomb of Khaemhat, superintendent of the granaries
Opposite below : Amenophis III in his war chariot with Nubian and negro prisoners of war

have been suggested as the reason. After seven requests Tuthmosis IV succeeded in marrying the daughter of Artatama, king of Mitanni; she became, it has been suggested, the mother of Tuthmosis's successor who, therefore, was half-Mitannian. This is interesting and for those who like genetic explanations for individual gifts and behaviour even attractive. But it is probably not true. Tuthmosis IV reigned only nine years. The negotiations were so protracted the marriage could not have taken place until towards the end of his reign and his successor, Amenophis III, would have been a mere baby. In fact he was old enough to marry. His mother's name is known; it was Mutemwiya, which is an Egyptian not a Mitannian name, and she came, Mr Aldred has argued, from a military family based at Akhmim, some 150 miles north of Thebes, which had close links with the royal family.

If Amenophis III was not half-Mitannian he was sufficiently different to attach no importance to the strong Egyptian tradition that a king should consolidate his legitimacy by marrying a princess of the blood royal. Perhaps one was not available. Amenophis married, as his Great Wife, an Egyptian commoner, as his father had, and was so proud of the fact that rather endearingly he issued scarabs, in much the same spirit as European monarchs have struck medals, to record that her name was Tiy, that her father's name was Yuia, her mother's name was Tjuia, and that she was 'the wife of a victorious king whose southern boundary is to Karoy [beyond Napata] and his northern to Naharin'. Her status, that is to say, depended on his status. As he was a god, it was implied that she was a goddess. This disregard of tradition is evidence of the strength and confidence of the Egyptian state, which was now at its zenith. His own mother was not a king's daughter and now he himself lacked what at one time had been thought essential, and would be thought essential again, a royal heiress for wife. Nobody seemed to care. They were all too well off to be exercised about such matters. In any case Tiy was the daughter of no ordinary noble. Her father Yuia, as will appear later, was also from the same Akhmim family; Queen Mutemwiya may have been his sister. This would make Amenophis III and Tiy cousins.

Amenophis III was the Louis Quatorze of Ancient Egypt. Both were Sun Kings, both reigned a long time, both were lovers of opulence and women. Amenophis was not a warrior (there was no need) though he did take pleasure early in life hunting lions and wild cattle. He loved big buildings and huge statues. The more colossal they were, the better. It was during his reign that the vogue for monster architecture really started. He loved food, jewellery, and the adulation of his people. He would have liked them to love him as a man but since that was impossible he insisted that they worship him as a god. His cult and that of Queen Tiy were handsomely endowed during their lifetimes. His Versailles was a palace covering eighty acres on the west bank of the Nile at Thebes called 'the Dwelling of Nebmare [which is his throne name], Re is Aten, a Shining Disc'. It was not architecturally distinguished by any means but consisted of a succession of buildings, some three storeys high with stairways to the roof, halls, and chambers enclosing courtyards and pleasure gardens. The material was mud-brick but plastered white and embellished with brilliant scenes of the good life – hunting game in the marshes, coursing antelope in the desert margins, and harpooning hippopotami in the lagoons of the Nile itself.

Queen Tiy had her own range of buildings. Just as there was no distinction between the sacred and the profane, there was no firm line dividing the domestic from the administrative; so here too were the Great Hall of the Vizier, where justice was dispensed, and the administrative departments of the Chancellor and Great Steward. To be the king's Butler was a high office of state; there were a number of these butlers and they had their establishments in the palace precincts. There was a quarter and courtyard for the royal harem. Wings were set aside for lesser queens who were daughters of Asian potentates. The king had his private temple on the site and one has the impression that visits to the great temple of Amon-Re at Karnak on the other side of the Nile were not so regular as they had been in earlier reigns. A post-meridian heat and silence seems to hang over the scene. Nubian guards snooze in the shade. A pet goose leaves the imperial bedroom where the king is taking his siesta and hisses at the baboon with the jewelled collar who scampers into the branches of a persea tree. Day after day the sultry heat and brilliant light came and faded. In the evening there would be a feast, music, and dancing. Under the very walls of the palace with torches flaring to keep away the midges and mosquitoes, Amenophis and the queen would be rowed on her pleasure lake in the cool of the night and in its pre-industrial silence.

Figures in ancient history now became human beings. They played roles, that is to say, and left personal records that allow us to re-create them in our imagination as flesh and blood. Maybe this re-creation is inaccurate but the evidence is of such a kind that a response is provoked peopling the ancient world with men and women we have at least the illusion of understanding. Tuthmosis III has been called the greatest of the Egyptian pharaohs but he lives in his heroic deeds; we lack the evidence of idiosyncracy that makes him a memorable 'character'. Perhaps that is why, in spite of his achievements, he is so little known. Queen Hatshepsut was clearly a woman of great ability and force of character but once again the quirks and oddities do not come through and we are left with speculations.

With Amenophis III and his Tiy we are in a different world. They were gods but it was a time when gods came down and walked with ordinary men and women. Amenophis was never more human than in his devotion to Tiy, who clearly dominated him. We know what she looked like. Her figure was slim and erect, her features fine and sensitive, and, in the fashion of the time, she wore a splendid wig that fell to her shoulders. Her grasp of politics was probably greater than her husband's. Foreign kings wrote to her direct. She is represented in statuary and in tomb paintings as fully the equal of Amenophis. She presided over his harem with the same care and efficiency great ladies supervised noble households in eighteenth-century Britain. She herself was prominently in evidence when foreign princesses arrived to occupy with their great retinues yet more wings in the palace as secondary queens. On the commemorative scarab prominence would be given not only to Amenophis and herself but to her parents Yuia and Tjuia as well, and the pleasure they took in the new arrival. This is what happened when Amenophis married Gilukhepa, daughter of King Shuttarna of Mitanni, who came with over three hundred attendants.

Compared with some ancient civilizations there is surprisingly little emphasis on sex in Egypt; in spite of obscene stories and cartoons they seem not to have been an overtly sensual people. There is no evidence of ritual prostitution as in Babylonia. But Amenophis had such an exceptionally large harem and took such obvious pleasure in adding foreign women to it that something other than political calculation clearly was at work. In the course of his reign he acquired the daughter of the new king of Mitanni, Tushratta, the sister (and then the daughter) of King Kadashman-Enlil of Babylon, plus the daughter of the king of Arzawa whose land was in the south-west of what is

Amenophis III and his queen, Tiy, from the Cairo Museum

now Turkey. A letter has survived from Amenophis to Milkili, the governor of Gezer in Canaan, sending silver in exchange for which he wanted forty women without blemish.

Negotiations for foreign princesses went on throughout his reign. To secure the Mitannian princess, Tadukhipa, the most experienced of the Egyptian ambassadors, a certain Mani, was sent to Shuttarna with presents and a letter inscribed in Akkadian carried, as was customary, in a wallet suspended from his neck. 'The gifts I send,' said Amenophis in this letter, 'are trivial compared with what I will send if you let me have the woman I want.' The travel-weary Mani had instructions from Amenophis not to be satisfied with anything but the best; if possible he was to inspect any woman offered by Shuttarna before a final decision was made. In the event all was well. Shuttarna allowed Mani to see his daughter Tadukhipa and the ambassador judged that she would excite his master's pleasure. In due course they set off for Egypt with another large retinue, a kind of portable chapel for the worship of one of the Mitannian gods, and the statue of a god capable of curing all manner of diseases.

When negotiating for a Babylonian princess, Amenophis found Kadashman-Enlil, the Kassite king, asking for an Egyptian princess in return. This Amenophis refused, saying that it was not the custom to allow Egyptian princesses to marry foreigners; meaning, but not saying so, that even he recognized that marriage to a royal princess constituted a claim to the double crown itself. Perhaps realizing this, Kadashman-Enlil said that he would be prepared to accept any woman, even if she was not a princess, provided she were beautiful; he could always pass her off as royal! But a more usual demand from Babylon was for gold. As the king of Babylon said to Amenophis, 'Gold is as common as dust in your country.' Queen Tiy, having a great international reputation for wisdom, would be party to all these negotiations and, while they lived, probably her parents too.

The great building programme undertaken by Amenophis III made Thebes into a metropolis that had no equal, not even at Babylon, in the ancient world. The city had a population of up to a million people and stretched for miles along the Nile. In the *Iliad* Homer refers to it as

Egyptian Thebes
Where all the houses have great treasure stored,
Thebes of the hundred gates, through each of which
Two hundred warriors sally with their teams
And chariots.

Only the temples were built of stone. Dwelling houses were of mud-brick and no doubt whole areas of the city consisted of one-storey dwellings fronting on to narrow streets where two laden donkeys could not pass without argument. It was a cosmopolitan city. Bearded Syrian soldiers and Cretans wearing patterned kilts jostled through the crowd. Blacks from the Sudan carried baskets of fruit and vegetables. Nubian policemen, almost as black but with thinner features and more prominent noses, paraded along a wider thoroughfare, watched curiously perhaps by rather fleshy traders from Babylonia. Men accustomed to the bleak uplands of Anatolia sweated in their woollen garments but did not care to walk about naked to the waist as so many Egyptians did. Tawny women from the banks of the Orontes, with long hair and ear-rings, pounded grain in the courtyards of their masters' houses. Everywhere children would be screaming at play or doing chores; for this was a young society where most died before middle age and even the better-off classes, where there was some expectation of longer life, regarded death as so ever-present that a tomb was considered and probably started as soon as a man had established himself in life.

A pharaoh of an earlier dynasty, Amenemhet I of the Twelfth, many centuries before Amenophis III, left his son some rather bitter advice. The king, he said, was of necessity lonely. 'Hold aloof from subordinates. Do not approach them in your loneliness. Fill not thy heart with a brother, know not a friend, nor create for thyself intimates.' The Middle Kingdom, from which that dates, was a simpler feudal world where power was less centralized and the king could be aloof and rule from a distance. Under the Eighteenth Dynasty Egypt was much more of a corporate state, with the king radiating lines of command through the various specialized authorities, the Viziers, the Chief Priest of Amon-Re, the army, the overseers of the Treasury and the Granaries. The administrative demands were great, so great that the king unless exceptionally intelligent and energetic could be manipulated by the specialists. In these circumstances it would be natural for him to turn to some general adviser whose job was to strengthen his judgement. Such people are sometimes called favourites and Queen Hatshepsut's Senenmut was one of these. For Amenophis III Queen Tiy herself played an important, perhaps dominant role as king's adviser, but so too did an official with the same name as the king who, to distinguish him, is therefore usually known as Amenhotep, son of Hapu. He was the greatest all-rounder of the age – scholar, architect, administrator, and general luminary. Contrary to the advice of the Twelfth Dynasty pharaoh, Amenophis III had a relationship with his namesake so renowned that centuries later it was preserved in a legend that in the course of one of their many conversations the king asked his favoured counsellor what could be done that he might actually see the gods.

A black diorite statue in Cairo shows Amenhotep, son of Hapu, at an advanced age (he lived to be eighty) in the traditional posture of the scribe, seated on the ground with an open papyrus sheet on his lap, with parallel folds of flesh across his belly and a quizzical, alert expression on his sharp features. It may have occurred to him that the king had a disconcerting way

The black diorite statue of Amenhotep, son of Hapu

of calling fundamentals into question without apparently really meaning to do so. See the gods? According to the legend the Great Scribe replied that the king should clear Egypt of its unclean people, its lepers, and then he would see the gods. The story is less important than the possibility that whoever concocted it did so out of a tradition that the king and his Great Scribe did indeed talk well into the night and that their conversation ranged widely. The son of Hapu was largely responsible for the organization of the king's first *Sed* festival, in the course of which, no doubt, he would explain what it all meant, why a particular honour was paid to one god and not to another. He might have said, in answer to the king's question, that there was a god seen daily, the sun. It would have been a courtly answer because Amenophis took pleasure in honouring the god that his father had honoured, the disc of the sun, Aten. There was an Aten temple in Thebes and the royal barge in which Amenophis sailed with Queen Tiy was called 'Aten Gleams'.

Amenhotep, son of Hapu, was responsible for the two seated statues of Amenophis III, seventy feet high, which are among the best known relics of Ancient Egypt, the Colossi of Memnon. He arranged for the quarrying of the red sandstone near Heliopolis, the carving of the two statues, their transport on barges to western Thebes, and their erection. Memnon is mentioned in the *Odyssey* as the son of Tithonus and Eos (the dawn) and the name was attached to the northerly of the two statues in Roman times because it greeted the dawn, its mother, with a melodious sound, a phenomenon that did not survive the restoration work of Septimius Severus. In their present ruinous condition these two statues are all that remain of the immense mortuary temple that once stood where the maize now grows. Amenophis III granted his namesake the highest honour pharaoh could confer – a mortuary temple of his own in western Thebes among the temples of the kings – and endowed it in perpetuity; not, one supposes, for such achievements as the erecting of the two colossal statues, but as public recognition that the son of Hapu was not only his greatest subject and a sage but his personal friend as well.

If, as seems likely, he was party to the king's ambitious programme of temple building, the wisdom of the son of Hapu was not of the kind that led to the telling of unwelcome truths. The resources of even this unprecedentally

Opposite : These massive seated statues of Amenophis III were originally in front of his funerary temple. In Ptolemaic times they became known as the Colossi of Memnon
Overleaf : At the height of the empire the governing classes under Amenophis III enjoyed a life of unexampled luxury and splendour
Top left : The daughter of Menna, Scribe of the Fields, during a fowling expedition. Bottom left : A banquet from the tomb of Nebamun. Top right : A horse and two mules in a harvesting scene. Bottom right : Goldsmiths and joiners at work

rich state were stretched. Other great temples, like Karnak, were built and added to by a succession of pharaohs but the temple of Luxor is mainly the responsibility of Amenophis III. His two principal architects were the same twin brothers, Suti and Hor, who composed the Hymn to the Sun.

Thou art a craftsman shaping thine own limbs;
Fashioner without being fashioned;
Unique in thy qualities, traversing eternity;
Over ways with millions under thy guidance.

But for all their personal predilections the Luxor temple is dedicated to Amon (it is his 'Harem of the South'), his wife Mut, and their son Khonsu. The Luxor and Karnak temples are the great monumental buildings of the time, the empire expressed in stone. Suti and Hor, who walked in pharaoh's procession when he appeared in public at the great festivals, would have seen their contribution not as an expression of any personal judgement they wished to exercise – Egyptian architects are normally as anonymous as their work is lacking in individuality – but as an expression of the spirit of the age.

Linking the Luxor temple to the main temple of Karnak was – and still is – a great processional way, with a row of ram-headed sphinxes on both sides, each of which has a small figure of the king between its paws. The temple of Amon itself received a new façade, the present fourth pylon; and in front of this pylon a start was made on the great hypostyle hall by building the central aisle of columns. To see this hall today with the sunlight flooding in through the broken roof is to gain a misleading impression of the feelings these brilliantly decorated and inscribed trunks of stone were meant to induce. In the half-light they stretched up to remote open or closed lotus-bud capitals. Priests between the great stems of these mimic plants walked like mice in a reed bed. The solemn procession of the god would at first seem reduced by the scale of the architecture against which it moved; and then, under the influence of incense clouds, the intoning of prayers, the tinkling of *sistra*, flute music, and the singing of women, the bearers would be exalted; gods and men mysteriously took on the stature of the giant vegetation that was now alive like the lotus and papyrus in the marshes. This stunning power house of imperialism, as it has been called, distended the imagination.

It was not completed by Amenophis III – that was left to later pharaohs – but the original concept dates from his time and it is the most grandiose statement of which the Egyptian empire, at its most opulent and confident, was capable. The prime mover in all this was without doubt Amenophis himself. If ever there was an emperor of the Ancient East it is he, but he sometimes

Opposite : The Great Court of the temple at Karnak showing an avenue of ram-headed sphinxes. The ram was the sacred animal of Amon, and this was the traditional way of marking a processional route

allowed himself to be presented in a way that surprises. On the one hand, it can be said, no pharaoh took his own godship more seriously. In his temple at Luxor there is a Birth Room where Amon-Re and the king's mother Mutemwiya are shown as consorts and the king's divine birth is depicted

The sandstone stela in the British Museum of Amenophis III relaxing with Queen Tiy

much as Hatshepsut's was across the river at Deir el-Bahri. He dedicated temples for the worship of Amon and of himself. Way up in Nubia he built a temple for the worship of Queen Tiy and himself. And yet, in spite of all these divine pretensions, he allowed himself to be portrayed as a very fallible man.

In art there was a new realism and naturalness at this time. Previously it was unheard of for pharaoh to be presented in an unflattering way; such treatment was only possible for peasants and foreigners. Yet a sandstone stela exists, now in the British Museum, which shows Amenophis in a most unkingly posture. He is clearly overweight, dressed in a low-necked effeminate gown and slumped in his chair with plump right arm hanging down and a hand dangling just below his knee. Queen Tiy is sitting with him and appears to be supporting him. His health is known to have deteriorated because he begged the loan of a wonder-working image from his brother-in-law, King Tushratta of Mitanni; it was of the goddess Ishtar of Nineveh and Tushratta asked for her back when her work was done – 'for she is not your goddess but mine'.

The only affliction we know Amenophis to have endured was toothache. His mummy reveals that he had large dental abscesses. But a god does not normally wish to be seen, even in a picture, being comforted by his wife. Elsewhere he is shown in a fringed dress with his hands clasped across his stomach, more like a Sumerian merchant than a pharaoh. No artist would have represented Amenophis in these ways without his approval. Perhaps he was too ill to care what people thought or maybe he disdained any opinion but his own. But a truthfulness about what the eye saw was in the Theban air in those days and the naturalism of his portraiture may argue no more than a fundamental honesty in the man. As for the femininity, that was fashionable. In spite of the underlying military strength the regime depended on, there was in art, costume, and jewellery a delicacy that seems to indicate women's tastes were prevailing.

In spite of the claim made at one of the temples where his cult was celebrated that he was the living image of god on earth, there is evidence, a little, of a basic simplicity in him that hints there is something substantial behind the legend that he wanted to see the gods – in the obscure and baffling hope, perhaps, that they would turn out worthier than he. It was a time when what seemed to be was not really so. And the contrary.

We know a surprising amount about the international diplomacy of the time because of the discovery at Tell el-Amarna in 1887 of part of the Foreign Office archives of Amenophis III and his immediate successors. They are in the form of clay tablets inscribed in the international language of the time, an archaic form of the Akkadian language of Mesopotamia. They consist mainly of communications from the vassal rulers in Syria–Palestine and from the kings of Mitanni, Babylon, Assyria, Alashia (in Cyprus), Arzawa, and, most important of all, the Hittite king, who at this time was an unusually able ruler called Shuppiluliumash. International relations in the Bronze Age East were, it turns out, more like those of eighteenth-century Europe than had previously been suspected.

The picture that emerges is of good and on the whole courteous communication at the international level. The kings of the different countries greeted each other as brothers and prefaced each letter with assurances that all was well in their country. Each hoped that all was well in his brother's country too, with particular reference to his wives, his chief men, his horses and his chariots. An international code of behaviour is revealed that was already antique. There were agreed procedures for handling criminals guilty of an offence in the territory of one monarch and who had escaped into the territory of another. If a foreigner died in Egypt his possessions would be sent to his next-of-kin in his homeland. Treaties of friendship provided not only for assistance against attack by third parties but forbade the support of a vassal against his lord. The king of Babylon refused to help the Canaanites against pharaoh because of his understanding with Egypt. Everywhere the king was regarded as responsible for law and order. If, as sometimes happened, the king of Babylon's caravan was plundered and his emissaries murdered in Palestine, which was internationally agreed to be Egyptian territory, then he expected from pharaoh the punishment of those responsible and compensation for his losses. After a successful campaign it was traditional for the victorious king to send some of the booty to his allies whether they had taken part or not. The health of monarchs was a matter of international concern. Presents were exchanged on a strict value-for-value basis. Gold was 'tested in the furnace' and short weight bitterly complained of.

Not only monarchs wrote to each other, their womenfolk did too. When Amenophis III died after reigning for thirty-nine years he was succeeded by his son Amenophis IV whose mother was Queen Tiy. Tushratta was so exasperated by the new pharaoh's behaviour that he wrote to his mother complaining that he had been fobbed off with wooden statues overlaid with gold by her son, Amenophis IV, when his deceased father – and alas! that he was deceased – had promised solid gold. 'Is this friendship?' he asked. One can imagine the expressive hunching of the shoulders and the raised hands as the king in his Washshukani palace dictated to the scribe. The new pharaoh seems to have irritated the king of Babylon in the same way. He had sent a present of gold but when Burnaburias melted it down and had it re-cast he found it less than had been promised. Please, he said to his brother, the king of Egypt, check the weight of the gold yourself. Don't leave it to an official.

By this time the Egyptians had given up any of the ambitions Tuthmosis III may have had for the control of northern Syria. Even he had recognized the limits of what was possible for the Egyptians in this area and made a treaty

of friendship with the Hittites. But where the Egyptians did see a continuing
interest was in the coastal area from Byblos up to the trading entrepôt of
Ugarit in the north. There were, however, a number of free-swimming
potentates in the area who might owe formal allegiance to pharaoh and even
have that allegiance recognized by the Hittites and Mitanni alike but who
nevertheless served their own interests first, even if it meant playing off one
great power against another. The chief example of such a man was the prince
of Amurru, a territory that was between Byblos and Ugarit, but inland. His
name was Abdi-Asurta and he made such a nuisance of himself, particularly
in the way he raided Byblos territory, that he was eventually murdered by a
detachment of Egyptian marines, specially detailed for the job. His sons,
particularly one called Aziru, were, if anything, even more aggressive than
their father. Aziru was summoned to Thebes and held there for some years
to undergo lessons in good behaviour, but when eventually he returned to the
mountains and pinewoods he transferred his allegiance to the new strong man
of the area, the Hittite king, Shuppiluliumash. If he wanted to stay alive he
probably had no alternative. Shuppiluliumash really did want to dispose of
Mitanni and control northern Syria. His arrival on the international scene
was the most important development in foreign affairs in Amenophis III's
reign and in spite of the treaties it led, many years later, to an open clash.

The chief victim of Amurru was Byblos, which at this time was ruled by a
certain Rib-Addi whose letters to pharaoh, his lord and Amurru's lord, were
long and frequent. The fact was that although Egypt did not want to see Rib-
Addi's territory swallowed up by Amurru, neither did pharaoh's advisers
wish to see Amurru so weak that it was no longer a check on Mitannian and
Hittite pressures. Egyptian policy was probably not at all well thought out;
in the end if failed because Amurru did in fact fall under Hittite control but
during the period of uncertainty, which lasted some years, Rib-Addi seems
slowly to have had the life squeezed out of him. His fate was all the more
tragic because his own brother was challenging him for control of Byblos
itself. During Rib-Addi's absence in Beyrout where he was negotiating an
alliance, this brother saw to it that the gates of Byblos were shut against him.
'If archers are not here this year,' he wrote to pharaoh, 'then send ships that
will take me with the living gods to my lord.' Later he wrote, 'I cannot now
come to the land of Egypt. I am old and my body is afflicted with a severe
disease.'

In southern Syria, including much of modern Lebanon and Damascus, and
Palestine, Amenophis III's suzerainty continued without serious challenge.
Rulers with Indo-European names sat in their fortified cities, all jockeying for
advantage and never hesitating to denounce each other to pharaoh for dis-
loyalty. While they wrote obsequious letters to their sovereign lord they were
actually plotting against each other and fighting petty wars. Egyptian com-
missioners saw to it that they paid tribute regularly. The harvests at Megiddo

and Sharon were stored in granaries. Just as in Egypt the Canaanite population did forced labour. Egyptian garrisons levied cattle, grain, and oil. The
Egyptian administrative centres were Joppa and Gezer, from which Egyptian
officials travelled out to make reports back to Thebes with their own evalua-
tion of the struggle between one vassal and another, a struggle that from the
Egyptian point of view might be thought to have advantages. Divide and rule.

Inevitably there was corruption. One regent complained that an Egyptian
official was actually holding Canaanites to ransom and demanding for their
release three times as much as ordinary bandits did. The repeated request
from the local regents was for troops, particularly archers, for defence against
other princes and the semi-nomadic tribesmen who, under the general name
of Habiru, raided cities and settlements, siding now with one and now the
other. Even when pharaoh did send troops they sometimes caused trouble.
At this time, before the Israelite conquest, the city of Jerusalem was built in
terraces on the sides of the valley of Kedron. Abdi-Hiba, the prince of Jerusalem, wrote and complained to pharaoh that Nubian archers had come down
the hillside, broken into his house through the roof, burgled it and almost
killed him in the process. 'May the king, my lord, my sun-god, avenge me.'

The Tell el-Amarna tablets from Palestine make it clear that the Habiru
were a major disruptive influence. The word 'Habiru' is the same as the word
'Hebrew' but it would be wrong to think the Habiru referred to in the tablets
were the Israelites under Joshua entering the Promised Land of Canaan. The
Israelites were undoubtedly Habiru, later on, but all Habiru were not Israelites. It was a general term, almost of abuse, for 'person from across or beyond'
and referred to people of mixed racial origin who spoke different languages.
A related word – perhaps it is the same – 'Apiru' meant 'dusty one' in reference
to the way they trudged behind donkeys on trading expeditions. There were
also *habbatu* or bandits and Beduin. Some of their chieftains rose to positions
of power. Labaya was an Apiru chief who gained control of an area between
Jerusalem and Megiddo. He wrote in Canaanite to pharaoh saying he fought
only when attacked. If pharaoh were to tell him to turn the other cheek, he
would not do so. 'I should still repel my foe.' This is unusually sturdy
language to address to 'the king, my lord' who in this particular letter is not
even referred to as 'sun-god'.

Seen from Thebes, however, these were trivial matters, of less interest to
many at the court than the style of a new wig or dress fashion. Imperial Egypt
flourished like the great persea tree Amenophis saw every morning from his
bedroom window.

6
AMARNA AND THE ECLIPSE OF AMON

ONE COULD REASONABLY HAVE EX-
pected Amenophis the Magnificent to be succeeded by a different kind of
pharaoh – one who, perhaps impatient of the restraints of peace and diplomacy, wanted to assert himself, act vigorously, and be a hero like his ancestors.
The new pharaoh was certainly different. No other pharaoh, before or after,
was at all like him, but the difference lies in his religious fanaticism, a most
un-Egyptian characteristic. Almost as though sceptical of finding truth lodged
in any one place, the Egyptians were an undogmatic people. Many-godded
societies do not go in for religious persecution. Amenophis IV did. He thought
he knew what the truth was and he acted on it. Yet when he died nothing of
what he tried to achieve survived. He was like a comet who came from
nowhere and then disappeared, leaving a trail that can be detected only in the
arts and, perhaps, a greater use in writing of more colloquial Egyptian. If the
Egyptian records from the time of Amenophis III to, say, twenty years after
the death of Amenophis IV had by some accident been totally lost, it would
have been impossible to deduce the existence of the kind of pharaoh he was.
Had he not been known to exist there would have been no need to invent him.
But as the records do exist he is the most written about of all pharaohs.

He was a bit like Shakespeare's Prospero, particularly in the way he neglected the affairs of state for intellectual pursuits. Unlike some medieval European monarchs all pharaohs were cultivated men who could read and write;
they had been trained as scribe and priest. The young man who now came to
the thrones of Egypt went further than this. He was not only a religious
thinker, he was an aesthete, a poet, a devoted family man, and, perhaps more
than anything else, an artist who was probably more at home in the studio
than anywhere else. With his encouragement and possibly under his direction, the first *avant-garde* artistic movement in history was launched. The
chief sculptor Bak described himself as the king's apprentice and claimed
that he worked to his instructions. The king also had an unusual appearance
of which he was seemingly proud and which he encouraged artists somewhat
to caricature in their portrait reliefs and statues. His physical appearance has
been attributed to a complaint known as Fröhlich's syndrome, a malfunction-
ing of the pituitary gland. At one extreme period his appearance was even

*Previous page : Akhenaten and Nefertiti worshipping the Aten, venerated
by Akhenaten not just as a solar disc but as the supreme god*

Amarna art developed an unprecedented freedom of line, naturalism, and realism. Here one of the royal princesses is shown eating a roast duck

attributed to his wife Nefertiti, their children, and courtiers. All had swollen thighs and abdomen, camel-like features, and egg-shaped heads. The religion he advocated was that of the sun-god, in the form of the sun disc, the Aten. To signify his repudiation of Amon and his devotion to the Aten, he changed his name from Amenophis ('Amon is satisfied') to Akhenaten ('he who is beneficial to Aten').

There is plenty of evidence that the Aten had its cult before Akhenaten took it up with such single-minded enthusiasm. And there are examples, too, before Akhenaten's reign of the freer, more spontaneous art that comes from trusting the eye rather than the brain. A word of caution is necessary here because no one is certain when Akhenaten's reign began. It is possible that he was co-regent with his father for the last eleven years of Amenophis III's reign and what we ascribe to a pre-Akhenaten regime may in fact be the product of it. Whether Akhenaten reigned with his father or not, there is no precedent for the calculated, even brutal realism of the portraiture. Art, for the Egyptians, was normally a magical activity that expressed their beliefs about the significance of life; although there were gifted artists and bad ones the difference would be seen in their ability to interpret the hallowed canons of art, certainly not in any failure to be original or pleasing. Individualism and what we would describe as purely aesthetic qualities were of less consequence to the Egyptians than orthodoxy. A departure from traditional art, such as we find in the time of Akhenaten, indicates a departure from traditional values.

Ma'at, or justice, was a concept of obviously great importance to Akhenaten.

Above : This carving dating from the reign of Akhenaten of soldiers emerging from a palace gives an impression of perspective new in Egyptian art. Opposite : The head of Akhenaten from a colossal statue now in the Cairo Museum

For him it came to mean not only the kind of justice that is a natural part of the right ordering of the universe, but justice in the sense of truth to observable fact. The intelligence might say that the representation of life should contain all the information we have about it – so that if we are painting a basket containing fifty bunches of grapes we should show each and every one of them balanced on top of a representation of the basket – but truth (in Akhenaten's sense) had a more innocent eye. The result was greater naturalism, the beginning of perspective drawing, animation, and what can almost be called impressionism in rendering landscape. Let us, Akhenaten seemed to be saying, break open the carapace of received opinion and convention and look at the world for ourselves. In our literature let us avoid archaisms and write more as we speak. It was unexpected, audacious, and so un-Egyptian that respected scholars of the period have said Akhenaten was mad.

What there was certainly no precedent for was his insistence that the gods, particularly Amon-Re, the god of the empire, were false gods. Only Aten was god. Even Osiris who, with Isis, had been at the centre of whatever was consoling in Egyptian religion was cast out. So determined was Akhenaten to make his point that he even abandoned Thebes. His father had lived, most of the time, on the other side of the Nile away from the great temple of Amon at Karnak but this was not distancing enough for his son, who moved away to the north and built an entirely new capital city where no city had been before, half-way between Thebes and Memphis. He called it Akhetaten, the Horizon of Aten. To build it, the wealth and resources of the temples of Amon and the other gods were sequestrated and a corps of workmen were sent round to chisel the name of Amon from all monuments, temple walls, stelae, and tomb inscriptions, even when it formed part of his own father's name. This had profound practical consequences. The sequestration of temple lands may have led, through lack of supervision in the handover from Amon to Aten, to a reduction of the cultivated area. Thousands of priests lost their occupation. There may have been a breakdown in food supplies – and this in as naturally fertile a land as Egypt! And yet, in spite of the cultural and political shock these innovations brought about, there is no evidence of any revolt against them. Even an unpopular pharaoh like Akhenaten was still complete master of all religious and secular life in Egypt. Defiance of Akhenaten would have been in the minds of the Amon priesthood but that was as far as it went. The power structure of the Egyptian state was tested to the point of destruction. The question is to what extent Akhenaten was making a purely religious onslaught on the existing state of affairs and to what extent he was reacting politically to the undoubted economic and political ascendancy of Amon by reasserting the authority of pharaoh. The Egyptian of the time

Opposite : The unfinished head of Nefertiti found in an artist's studio at Tell el-Amarna

would not have thought about the question in this analytical way but that does not mean, with the limited evidence we have, that we should dodge the issue.

Akhenaten, one guesses, might have thought the priesthood of Amon were taking too much on themselves but the dogmatism, even the bigotry, of which he was capable seems to indicate a spiritual basis for his actions. He was going back to basics. The ancient religion of Egypt was unquestionably the sun religion and in returning to it he was simply reaffirming ancient perceptions and ancient truths. The real religion, one can imagine him arguing, had always been monotheistic and the multiplicity of cults now observable in the land were mere concessions to fallible human beings who, lacking guidance, naturally took limited views which ended up in their worshipping some purely local god like Sobek, the crocodile-god, or perhaps more understandably even great Amon of Thebes. The true godhead was more abstract. Akhenaten was no political manoeuverer. He was acting on what he considered a matter of principle. His predecessors had created a centralized state of such strength that resistance to his reforms would have been difficult to organize. There were no barons, only, perhaps, troublesome priests and Akhenaten now reminded them that constitutionally he was god on earth.

The cast of Akhenaten's mind has been described as a not unexpected consequence of the international thinking of the empire. There was a need to escape from provincial concepts of power and divinity to a concept that would have appeal to all men, irrespective of their race. The fanaticism has been seen as Asiatic. No man is an island. The intellectual climate of the time may well have nudged men away from thinking relativistically about revealed truth in favour of some more comprehensive dogma. But Akhenaten showed little interest in maintaining Egypt's international position. His Atenism made no overt appeal to foreigners. He seemed so confident of the fabric of the new intellectual world he was creating that ordinary calculations of power and wealth did not matter.

The cult image of Amon-Re in his shrine at Karnak was removed by Akhenaten's agents and smashed. The only other possibility would have been its secret removal and concealment in, say, some obscure grave shaft in the cliffs of western Thebes, the god becoming 'the Hidden One' in the literal sense until better times returned. Akhenaten's agents were, however, busy with their hammers and the image at the centre of the proscribed cult would be an obvious victim. For the priesthood of Amon it was an almost unimaginable sacrilegious horror to witness the doors of the shrine opened by the profane and unpurified agents of the king; then, by the light of torches, to see the striding figure of the god thrown on a pile of sand and hammered, his obsidian eyes put out and the blue head struck from his body. The temples stood empty, fell into disrepair, and weeds sprang up wherever the soil was damp enough. For the worship of the Aten the temples of Amon were useless. A sun-god did not want a dark sanctuary but an offering table in an open court-yard where the god in his rising and transit across the sky could preside in person. The gold, the silver, the bronze, the precious stones, hangings, and furnishings of the temples were ferried to Akhetaten. Concealment of wealth or cult images was severely punished. Anyone suspected of it was tortured, usually by the bastinado.

Akhenaten did not have a Hymn of Victory as his ancestor Tuthmosis III had. Instead, like Francis of Assissi, he composed his own Hymn to the Sun. It was by no means the first such hymn. The architects Suti and Hor composed one in his father's time; another earlier hymn, preserved on papyrus, has the same warm-hearted response as Akenaten's Hymn to the beneficence of the great sun-god whose love extended to all living things. Akhenaten was writing within an existing tradition, but he contributed a praise of Aten's creativity that anticipates G. M. Hopkins in its exuberance. With the Jesuit poet Akhenaten would have said, 'Glory be to God for dappled things.' What he actually wrote was imbued with feeling. 'All goats skip on their feet, all that fly take wing. . . . The fish in the stream leap before thy face. . . . When the chick comes forth from the egg to chirp with all his might he goes upon his two legs, thanks to the breath thou hast given it. . . . How manifold are thy works.'

When Akhenaten's Hymn is set side by side with Tuthmosis' Hymn of Victory the change that had come over Egyptian thinking as a result of a comparatively peaceful possession of empire for so long can be seen for itself. Leaving aside the difference of tone, formal in the Victory Hymn, warm, even passionate in Akhenaten's, there is a real difference of content. Whereas Tuth-mosis spoke of 'wretched foreigners' and the humiliations he was able to impose on them, Akhenaten spoke of the foreign lands of Syria and Kush where, just as in Egypt itself, every man was blessed by the sun-god and enjoyed his own place in life. For the benefit of Asiatics he put 'a Nile in the sky' – gave rain, that is to say. Men speak different languages, have different traditions and customs, but all this is to the greater glory of god. Let us praise him for variety, difference, and the way he has distinguished the nations from one another.

It sounds like a creed designed for export but in reality it had no popular following even in Egypt itself, let alone elsewhere. Akhenaten seems to have been no more interested in proselytizing than any other pharaoh. Atenism was a court religion and little more. It was a personal enthusiasm. If he had decided there was to be no god but himself, the cult of Aten is what he would have set up. God, the Aten, was the impersonal disc of the sun and Akhenaten claimed that he was the incarnation of that deity. It followed that there was no higher authority in this life or the next but pharaoh himself. Akhenaten did not actually present himself as sole creator god in this way but it seems that is what he took to be the truth. The Aten creed was the nearest he could get to such a claim that was in a manner acceptable to his contemporaries and, indeed, to his own conscience. Although the Egyptian word for 'bow' translates as 'to sniff the ground', the traditional bow to pharaoh had previously been little more than a pronounced inclination of the body. But now, in deference to his pretentions, courtiers were for the first time depicted prostrating themselves and really sniffing the ground before Akhenaten as not just the 'good god' but the supreme and unique god. In art the Aten is shown as just a disc but with the royal uraeus fixed to it as though it were a king. The rays it sends out end in hands holding the *ankh* symbol of life and the *uas* sceptre of power. The clearest indication of the identity of Akhenaten and the Aten is their simultaneous celebration of the *Sed* festival as a common jubilee.

The tradition out of which Akhenaten's Hymn came dates back to the fifteenth century BC. It was still alive some six or seven hundred years after Akhenaten and in another language. The parallels between the Aten Hymn and Psalm 104 are well known. In both the lion is described going out to hunt when darkness falls. At the rising of the sun men rise and go out to their labour. 'O Jehovah,' says the Hebrew psalmist, 'how manifold are thy works. In wisdom thou has made them all; the earth is full of thy riches.' Akhenaten wrote, centuries before, 'How manifold are thy works; one and only God thou hast made the earth to thy desire.'

The link is not a direct one from Egyptian into Hebrew. The Canaanites had developed an alphabet out of Egyptian writing and adapted a wealth of Egyptian hymns, meditations, and even love songs, which in turn were imitated by writers in Hebrew. This cultural transfusion is the most attractive evidence we have for the beneficent flow of ideas across ethnic frontiers in the Egyptian empire. The Song of Songs itself is rooted in even more ancient love songs from the Nile valley.

The site of Akhetaten today is largely desert beyond the modern village of El-Till, which draws its life from the cultivated land along the eastern bank of the Nile. Beyond the palm groves are heaps and mounds masking the foundations of the temples and palaces, all on a huge scale but hurriedly built, as though under the impatient urgings of Akhenaten himself. During the building it must have looked like a very dusty antheap. The ox-carts that brought in stone from the neighbouring hills raised great billows of fine sand. At the newly constructed quays craft from Memphis and Thebes tied up with cargoes of masonry, furniture, the plunder of temples, chariots with their horses, the state archives, and a vast amount of slave labour. All the buildings of a great administrative centre can still be identified – the various equivalents to such modern ministries as the Office of Works, the Vizier's Broad Hall which was the Ministry of Justice, a Records Office, barracks and warehouses. Fine houses for senior officials gave on to broad thoroughfares. Lesser officials and merchants occupied a northern quarter adjacent to the Nile quays. Like Thebes and Memphis it was a cosmopolitan city. One of the smaller houses was clearly occupied by a foreigner from Crete or Mycenae. It was less formal than an Egyptian house. The fruit trees were dotted about, not in lines, and the staircase to the roof was open, supported, that is to say, not with a blank wall but with a square pier as in the Greek world.

In the cliffs of the eastern hills the rock tombs of high officials like the 'Father of the God', Ay, tell us most of what we know about the daily life of the city. The great temple of the Aten had no Holy of Holies but a huge round-topped stela in a courtyard open to the sky, with representations of Akhenaten, his wife Nefertiti, and their daughters at their devotions. Nefertiti's sensitive face is familiar to us because of the well-known polychrome head in the Berlin Museum and the even more striking, dream-like, unfinished head found in the remains of an Amarna studio and now in the Cairo Museum. Her name means 'a beautiful woman has come' and some have taken this to mean she was of Mitannian origin. As Mr Aldred has shown, the real story of Nefertiti and her family is even more interesting.

The new centralized Eighteenth Dynasty state had created the need for functionaries who were both loyal to pharaoh and of outstanding ability. Men who had distinguished themselves on active service or in administration became butlers and stewards of pharaoh's household. A Master of the Horse, a military rank, would become the confidant of pharaoh. Increasingly foreigners, through sheer ability and hard work, achieved high position; later a Nubian would advance to such a high dignity as that of Fan Bearer on the King's Right Hand. But in the earlier reigns of the Eighteenth Dynasty the really personal support for 'the good god' came from certain families who not only had the trick of providing a meritocracy but had beautiful daughters as well to marry into royalty. The outstanding family was the one that Queen Tiy came from, the Yuia family of Akhmin, a hundred miles to the north of Thebes.

There is strong circumstantial evidence that this family played a more important part in the family relationships of the dynasty and therefore in the history of Egypt than was thought before 1903. In that year the nearly intact tomb of Queen Tiy's parents was discovered. Although the mummy of Tjuia, the queen's mother, showed her to be a lady with the rather rounded features of some Egyptians, the mummy of Yuia showed that he was a tall man with long white hair, a nose as beaked as the Tuthmosids, and full, rather fleshy lips – an appearance, that is to say, not particularly Egyptian. From whom, one wonders did Amenophis II inherit his unusually great stature? Certainly not from his father Tuthmosis III. If Meryetre-Hatshepsut was not a daughter of Queen Hatshepsut herself was she a scion from the Akhmin family? Possibly. If the involvement of the family with royalty really did go back a long way it would explain much that is at present obscure. The tall, white-haired father of Queen Tiy was known as 'Father of the God' – this was part of the valuable information provided by the tomb – which at this period usually meant that his daughter was married to pharaoh. As indeed Queen Tiy, his daughter, was. But his own father, a certain Yey, was also 'Father of the God'; it has been surmised that Yuia's own sister was married to pharaoh too, and this could only be Mutemwiya, wife of Tuthmosis IV.

All this is based on information culled from the tomb of Queen Tiy's parents and if it sounds complicated then we can add to the complication by saying that in the next generation a prominent figure at the court of Akhenaten was yet another Yuia. He is usually referred to as Ay but Egyptian writing indicated only the consonants and the names are really the same. This Ay also came from Akhmin. He had exactly the same jobs as Queen Tiy's father. They were Master of the Horse, Divisional Commander, Fan Bearer on the King's Right Hand, and so on. The Egyptian expectation was that jobs would be inherited and clearly Yuia and Ay were father and son. The second Yuia, or Ay, was also 'Father of the God'. The only pharaoh to whom he could be father-in-law was Akhenaten. His Chief Wife was Nefertiti.

Ay, Yuia before him, and Yey before him were therefore not just prominent nobles. They may well have been of royal descent, their daughters became queens of Egypt, and one of them, Ay, eventually ascended the throne himself. At a time when family ties were particularly strong and successive pharaohs delighted in demonstrating the love they had for their respective Chief Wives – none more so than Akhenaten – the influence of the Akhmin family must have been great indeed. There is no evidence that they had the slightest influence on Akhenaten's religious and artistic radicalism. Queen Tiy visited Akhetaten and must have been puzzled, if not distressed, by the uncompromising monotheism of her son. By all means, one can imagine her saying, make the Aten your particular cult but please don't neglect the other gods. It would not be understood. It would not be Egyptian. It was not *Ma'at*. It would certainly have upset your father.

How did the new city of Akhetaten look from Syria and Palestine? The vassals and regents were frankly perplexed. The city of Tunip complained of neglect. 'In the time of Tuthmosis III,' the citizens wrote, 'anyone threatening Tunip would have been plundered by the king. Now Tunip weeps.' The regents of Byblos, Jerusalem and other key cities wrote for support. They did not ask for much. Rib-Addi of Byblos never asked for more than six hundred infantry to defend him against Amurru, and Pirywaza of Damascus pleaded for only two hundred men. The general impression in Retenu was that pharaoh was preoccupied with other matters and neglecting threats to his power. The letters from the vassal princes repeatedly strike a note of incomprehension. Does not pharaoh understand that his vital interests are involved? Unless he acts does not pharaoh see that his authority will count for nothing here? It is unlikely that appeals for help from the vassals went entirely unheeded if only for the reason that they continued for so many years. Punitive

Nefertiti playing with her daughters. Domestic scenes of this
intimacy involving the royal family were previously unknown

forces were sent repeatedly but not on a scale needed to establish a real Egyptian peace. The will did not exist.

Akhenaten delighted in the good life. He was demonstrative of his affection for his Chief Wife and children; the scenes of royal domesticity, the queen seated on the king's lap, the girls playing and talking in the presence of their indulgent parents, are of a kind not to be found anywhere else in Egyptian art. Whereas Amenophis II delighted in shooting arrows at copper targets while driving at a gallop, Akhenaten preferred to be shown in his chariot embracing his wife. If Nefertiti had born him a son, which she did not, we might have seen a new holy triad on the pattern that came so naturally to

Egyptians. Osiris, Isis, and Horus were the most ancient trinity; Amon, Mut, and Khonsu were the trinity of the empire. Akhenaten did the best in the circumstances. Nefertiti became not just Chief Wife but a kind of goddess-pharaoh with the name of Nefer-neferu-Aten ('Fair is the goodness of Aten') and was shown on a panel in the cabin of her state barge as a conquering pharaoh in a special tall hat clubbing an Asiatic foe. Akhenaten, for all his reputation as a pacifist, was likewise shown in the traditional warrior role, though it is highly unlikely he ever did anything more athletic than hunting, which he enjoyed. After Nefertiti's death their daughter Meryt-Aten assumed her mother's role and title. It must have been a time of anxiety about the succession. The Holy Family in Akhetaten desperately needed a son and Nefertiti's failure to provide one must, in the traditional oriental way, have been a source of grief and shame to her.

Round about the twelfth year of Akhenaten's reign a breakdown in his new order seems to have been acknowledged by the king himself. It is tempting to suppose this was at the prompting of his widowed mother, who must have been increasingly alarmed at the way things were going. Neither Akhenaten nor his Vizier Nakht had the administrative genius to reform the economy in a way consistent with the new concentration of power at Akhetaten. No doubt corruption was endemic in Egypt and it would be unfair to attribute all the abuses of the time to Akhenaten; but there does seem to have been confusion about who exactly was responsible for what. While Akhenaten was living by *Ma'at* in his pleasure city, elsewhere in Egypt it was often every tax-gatherer and local military commander for himself, commandeering slaves, crops, timber, cattle, and ships for his own use. Magistrates were so ill paid that if corrupt officials were charged they were open to bribery. There was more criminal extortion in the client territories of Palestine and Syria. The regent of Gezer had to complain that the Egyptian commissioner, Iankhamu, had seized his wife and children to reinforce his demand for two thousand pieces of silver. The occupying troops were hated for the way they helped themselves to whatever they fancied. All this fraud meant that the centralized state was not adequately financed and one wonders whether even the gangs of workmen at Akhetaten itself always received their rations on time. In such circumstances the naming of Akhenaten's eventual successor would be a matter of wide public concern. A youth called Smenkhkare was appointed co-regent by Akhenaten and he appeared to be not the totally con-vinced Atenist that current orthodoxy required. He is known to have pre-pared a tomb for himself in the traditional necropolis at Thebes – a political gesture of some importance – and since this could have been done only with the approval of Akhenaten, it has been taken as evidence of the king's recog-nition that there was a need for *rapprochement* with the priestly hierarchy of Amon.

There is too much uncertainty about chronology and personalities to be

The alabaster head of Smenkhkare from the top of a canopic vase

confident about what was going on. Smenkhkare's background is obscure. If Akhenaten had been co-regent with his father Amenophis III for a sufficient number of years, then the supposed years of his independent reign would be telescoped and it would have been possible for Smenkhkare to be, like himself, the son of Amenophis III and Queen Tiy. Similarly the next pharaoh, Tutankhamon. Or they could be the sons of Amenophis III by his daughter Sitamun. Or they could be Akhenaten's sons by a secondary queen. Or Akhenaten was impotent and even the daughters were not his. Research of this kind has, no doubt, a fascination of its own, but whatever its findings turn out to be, they can have no significance compared with the fact that the reign of Akhenaten coincided with domestic confusion at home and a sharp decline in Egyptian power over Syria–Palestine and possibly over Nubia too.

Smenkhkare was given Nefertiti's title of Nefer-neferu-Aten, which means that either she had died or had fallen into disgrace and, as some scholars put it, was replaced by Smenkhkare in Akhenaten's favours. The two kings were certainly shown on a stela in an affectionate embrace. But their time was short. Smenkhkare probably died before the older king. Even if he did not, the last years of Akhenaten must have been marked by a succession of painful bereavements, none more so than that of his daughter, Meketaten, whose death occasioned such grief in Akhenaten and Nefertiti that it was thought proper, in a quite unprecedented way, to show them in a relief at the royal tomb at El-Amarna mourning over her bier. Art did not normally reveal pharaoh so intimately. It is for such touches, almost as much as for his battle for monotheism against the entrenched interests of Amon, that he is referred to as the first individual in history.

Akhenaten died in 1362 BC after a reign of some eighteen years and was succeeded either immediately or soon after by a boy of nine, probably a younger brother of Smenkhkare, who was known first of all as Tutankhaten and later, as part of the general conciliation with the old religions, Tutankhamon. The court transferred not, as might have been expected, to the imperial city of Thebes but downstream to the more ancient capital of Memphis, almost as though 'the Father of the God', Ay, who was now the real power behind the throne, thought a wary distance between battered orthodoxy and the new pharaoh was still advisable.

Tutankhamon in his brilliantly painted state barge would be rowed north with the current by relays of oarsmen, the boy pharaoh climbing to the roof of the cabin from time to time for a better view. His wife, the royal princess Ankhesenpaaten, was older than Tutankhamon, perhaps by as much as ten years. She would have had no interest in such undignified scampering about and probably remained out of the sun in the seclusion of her cabin. A flotilla of lesser barges and ships fanned out behind, rowed from first light to sunset. Nobles with their families, their treasure, their household goods, each in his own craft, went north with an expectation of a very different life. Clearly the great migration was not carried out in one great expedition. Ships and barges would be shuttling between Akhetaten and Memphis for months, perhaps even years, transporting workshop equipment, papyrus records, statues, furniture, wooden pillars that would now support new roofs in Memphis or elsewhere, and even the dead. The royal mummies went to Thebes and lesser mummies to family burying places where, as would no longer be possible at the abandoned Akhetaten site, there would be guards to prevent the plundering of the tombs. Court records that were obsolete and could not easily be destroyed, like some of the clay tablets in the Foreign Ministry, were buried, not to be dug up again for well over three thousand years. The city was not entirely abandoned but no building of any consequence was ever put up on the site again. This is why its remains provide an almost unique example of the layout of an Ancient Egyptian city.

Because he had been so prominent at the court of Akhetaten and was now instrumental in the dismantling of his new order, Ay, who was now Vizier, has been described as an unscrupulous opportunist whose real ambition was to seize power for himself. He had certainly been high in royal favour as the king's father-in-law. It was in his tomb that Akhenaten's Hymn to the Sun was inscribed in its most complete form. Ay was unmistakeably identified with Atenism. Yet now as Vizier and probably co-regent he had advised Tutankhamon to make his peace with Amon. He was the leading member of the Akhmim family and that provided him with a special angle on the realities of power.

The material is flimsy but a case could be made out for Ay being the Talleyrand of Ancient Egypt, a political realist mainly activated by what he regarded as the country's best interests. Having served Napoleon, Talleyrand saw the Bourbons as the only solution to the French problem. The strength and well-being of Egypt, Ay seemed to have decided, depended on the kind of legitimacy represented by the house of Amosis (of whom Tutankhamon seems to be the last male descendant) and a re-establishment of the many gods of Egypt, particularly Amon-Re. The opinions held by those who mattered were that all misfortunes at home and abroad could be ascribed to neglect of the gods, and Ay would have seen how isolated Akhenaten had become. His pretensions had been gigantic. To paraphrase Talleyrand, Ay might have said, 'With a return to the gods, Pharaoh, who is Egypt, will cease to be gigantic in order to be great.'

The accession of a child like Tutankhamon to the thrones of Egypt at a time of near economic breakdown must have been viewed with great apprehension. If the Queen Dowager Tiy was still alive she and her brother Ay between them would have been the chief formers of policy. If it is the case, as has recently been argued (notably by Mr Aldred), that she was the mother of Smenkhkare and Tutankhamon, she would have seen three of her sons wearing the double crown and observed the high summer of empire pass. Princess Sitamun, another daughter of Queen Tiy whom Amenophis III actually married, occupied a great palace of her own at Akhetaten and played a shadowy part in these great events, maybe even a crucial one if only the evidence could be found. She, too, has been suggested as the mother of Smenkhkare and Tutankhamon. A lot depended on the success of the boy pharaoh and sacrifices were made to the gods that his reign might be long. No one was more sincere in this wish than Ay himself, even though political necessity required that he should be declared Crown Prince designate until such time as Tutankhamon and his Chief Queen had a son.

It is customary to talk of Ay as an old man but he was probably no more than fifty at the accession of Tutankhamon. His was undoubtedly the mind behind the statement of the new king now made on a stela at Karnak. Just as Hatshepsut before him had claimed to be a great restorer of temples, so Tutankhamon now described how they had become overgrown with weeds, how the sacred places had become public footpaths, and the whole land desolate because the gods had been neglected. In candour that was rare for a pharaoh he said there had been military failure in Asia. Now all was to be changed, the old faiths restored, the gods replaced in their sanctuaries, priests inducted, the king's own slaves purified for service in the temples as singers and dancers, and Amon-Re himself would sail once more on his sacred barque to the Harem of the South for the Feast of Opet. The Karnak stela is not specific about policy in Asia but General Horemheb was soon leading a powerful expeditionary force there, 'to slay the Asiatics in the field' and set the stream of tribute flowing as of old.

All seemed to go well. Ambitious building work at Thebes and in Nubia was undertaken, a sure sign that economic stability was returning. Horemheb was brilliantly successful in Palestine. It was as though the glorious days of empire were back again and the years of the heretic pharaoh could be buried and forgotten. The young Tutankhamon showed himself possessed of a vigour and interest in military affairs that promised well for the future. Only some unforeseen disaster would see Ay playing a more significant part than that of Vizier. But that disaster occurred when Tutankhamon died at the age of about eighteen. It is customary to say that the cause of his death is unknown, but his mummified head shows a puncture wound near his left ear. There is no certainty whether it occurred before or after death. If before it would be astonishing. Assassinations were not normally carried out by stabbing a man in the side of the head; had Tutankhamon died in this way the only conceivable perpetrator of such a deed would have been Ay, and an understanding of Egyptian history at this time does not require a monster of that kind. Another possibility would be that the blow was received either accidentally or in battle, in which case Tutankhamon would be was the first pharaoh to die in combat since Seqenenre two hundred years before. But the probability is that he died of natural causes.

He is famous because of his tomb, which was discovered by Howard Carter in 1922 more or less intact, with all its grave furnishings, its shrines, its gold masks, its jewels, its furniture, and its undisturbed mummy of the king himself. The splendour of the Tutankhamon treasures has aroused, broadly speaking, two reactions. If these are the funerary treasures of an obscure pharaoh, what would have been found in the tomb of an undeniably great one like Tuthmosis III or a really opulent one like Amenophis III? The other reaction was to say that the Tutankhamon treasure is so spectacular because there was a wish on the part of the priests of Amon and the rest of the temple hierarchy throughout Egypt to demonstrate their devotion to the pharaoh under whose reign the old religious order had been re-established. But neither of these reactions is quite right.

The main reason for the extraordinary wealth of objects in the small tomb (one not originally intended for Tutankhamon but forced upon Ay by un-expected necessity) was that they consisted in part of treasure intended for the tombs of Smenkhkare and Akhenaten but not used. Akhenaten could not have been buried in the splendour of the old Osiris religion because he had proscribed it. Smenkhkare too, if he died as seems likely before Akhenaten, had a funeral that was arranged in accordance with the rather austere views that pharaoh took of the future life. So Tutankhamon, the last in the line of the dynasty that had liberated Egypt from the Hyksos, inherited in death the tribute intended for his two royal predecessors and, no doubt, the evidence that Ay wished to provide of his sense that a great era had come to an end and that a new one was beginning.

The reaction of Ankhesenpaaten (her name changed to Ankhesenamon for political reasons) to the death of her young husband was extraordinary. She was in her late twenties, the daughter of one pharaoh and the widow of an-other, with no son to assume the double crown under her guidance, as Akhenaten had in his early years been guided by Tiy. Although Ay was for-mally the Crown Prince she had never taken this pretension in an elderly man with any seriousness. He was her subject and, as it happened, her grandfather. The only way his assumption of the kingship could be properly legitimized was through marriage with her, and this, Ankhesenamon decided, was out of the question. Indeed, she saw no one in Egypt who could be her husband so her thoughts turned to Asia. She wrote to Shuppiluliumash, king of the Hittites, saying that she understood he had many sons. Would he not send her one? She would marry him and make him king of Egypt.

Shuppiluliumash must have received this surprising letter at Hattushash very soon after he had heard of Tutankhamon's death. The Hittites were the rising, if not the risen, power in the north and a formal alliance between them and Egypt would have signalled the parcelling up of much of the civilized world. It was a bold and attractive idea – so attractive to Shuppiluliumash that he thought it might be an Egyptian trick. He sent an envoy to find out exactly what was going on. Time was short. The negotiations were taking place in the seventy days interregnum between the death of a pharaoh and his formal internment. The envoy returned with the information that Queen Ankhesenamon meant precisely what she said. A Hittite would rule in Egypt. Shuppiluliumash hesitated no longer. He sent his son Zannanzash and the unfortunate young man was murdered, presumably on Ay's instructions, *en route*, in Palestine.

Ankhesenamon's idea would never have worked. So Ay would have advised had she consulted him. How could a Hittite be Chief Priest to the Egyptian pantheon? There was no knowing which way a foreign pharaoh would take Egypt. What the country needed, Ay decided, more than anything after the Amarna heresy was a period of stability and consolidation. This palace struggle was going on behind the scenes while the Tutankhamon treasures were being moved into his tomb. Inevitably, Ankhesenamon and her faction lost because of an understanding between the Vizier Ay and General Horemheb. The oracle of Amon indicated that there was no alternative to Ay becoming pharaoh himself, regularizing his position as divine monarch by marrying Ankhesenamon, and appointing Horemheb his heir. Horemheb was already married to Ay's daughter Mutnodjme – a sister of Nefertiti and presumably much like her – so he was the inevitable successor.

Horemheb succeeded his father-in-law after four years, in 1349 BC, and reigned for thirty years. He must be accounted among the most able administrators the country ever had. He regarded himself as a legitimate king in the dynasty that had ruled for the previous two hundred years and indeed he may have had a more direct royal descent than we know of. In Tutankhamon's time he had been an indefatigable traveller throughout the length and breadth of the country, dealing with the local lawlessness that, as an inheritance from Akhenaten's time, was all too prevalent. What was remarkable about Horemheb was the way he questioned the system from the top down, particularly the part played by royal favourites in the administration of the country. All his instincts were against these personal and sometimes quite arbitrary appointments.

His reforms were published as an edict on a large stela at Karnak about five metres high and three wide. It tells how the king took his writing palette and papyrus roll to set down what he would do 'to expel evil and suppress lying' and so seek 'the welfare of Egypt'. Then follow enactments to restrain officials and soldiers from seizing goods and services for their own use. The penalties were harsh, out of proportion to the offences sometimes, rather as though in the new bureaucracy written regulations were taking over from more personal authority, from pharaoh's down, and it was intended to make these regulations of exemplary severity. A frequent punishment was the cutting off of the nose and exile to Tjel, the frontier fortress at the beginning of the road to Palestine across the Sinai desert. Horemheb's main displeasure was for those who diverted to their own use imposts and dues intended for pharaoh himself; but he went out of his way to emphasize that a poor man who is robbed must have his goods restored. In a section dealing with indiscipline among soldiers, he reaffirmed the organization of the Home Command in two armies, one centred on Thebes, the other on Memphis. During Akhenaten's time the organization may have fallen into disuse and needed re-establishing to ensure firmer control of the troops from the top. Full judicial and administrative responsibility was returned to the two Grand Viziers, one for Upper, the other for Lower Egypt, and magistrates were to be paid properly so that they were less tempted to take bribes. If they did it was a capital offence.

Horemheb as pharaoh making an offering

The administrative weakness of Akhenaten's regime had been centraliza-
tion without effective delegation. Horemheb saw the weakness and made his
two Viziers, his two army commanders, and the Chief Priest of Amon responsible to him for the powers he now took care to see they had. But unlike
the Viziers and the army commanders, the powers of the Chief Priest were
not divided. Making all allowances for the difference between the priestly
authority of Karnak and the kind of authority enjoyed by the Viziers, pri-
marily judicial, and the army commanders, nevertheless Horemheb had confirmed the Chief Priest, the supreme pontiff of all Egyptian cults, in the only
unitary command that could be compared with his own. Because he restored
the privileges and wealth of the hierarchy, Horemheb alone, of all the great
figures of the Amarna period, was recognized by his successors and by the
Amon priesthood as legitimate. To quote the edict: 'The king appointed the
priests to judge the citizens of every city.' After the years of humiliation
Amon-Re was now back in the ascendant.

Horemheb was a great talker. When still a general he had cut for himself a
tomb (it was never used) in Saqqara which has an inscription ascribing part
of his success in life to his eloquence. Egyptians admired the articulate
speaker. One of the most popular of all old stories was that of the eloquent
peasant who had been robbed and argued for justice through a series of
appeals. He won his case, and the manner of his doing so, by invoking *Ma'at*
as that fundamental good pharaoh and peasant alike must acknowledge,
gained him the favour of the very Chief Steward whom in his pleading he had
attacked. The story goes back to an earlier period in Egyptian history, the
Middle Kingdom, but Horemheb would have known it and, judging by his
edict, wished to create a society where once again an appeal to justice, particularly if presented with wit and courage, would prevail against the jack in
office. Even under a fair-minded ruler such as he, the system was nevertheless
a repressive one. Order was restored at a price. Part of the price was what now
happened at Karnak. Amon-Re was out sailing in his barque again and the
sacerdotal power he exercised seemed, mysteriously, to generate more power
without any help from the priests. Akhenaten's great gesture was not only
forgotten, but out of shame and guilt it was repressed into some gulf of the
national consciousness. Even the hard-headed Horemheb could not see that
by compensating Amon-Re for the indignities he had suffered, he was in any
way modulating the power structure of Egypt. The Chief Priest of Amon,
he would have said, was his man, to be appointed or removed at his pleasure.
Nevertheless Amon who had been great was, by unperceived degrees, becoming greater.

7
THE RAMESSIDE
REACTION

THE DYNASTIES WERE RECORDED BY
Manetho, who worked in Alexandria during the third century BC and whose
history has now largely been lost. His king-lists remain and although much
corrected by historians still have value as a point of reference. Horemheb was
followed by a king it is customary to regard as the first of a new dynasty, the
Nineteenth, because he was not a descendant of Amosis nor, like Horemheb,
had he married into the family, though about this there is no certainty.
Ramesses I had been Vizier and the King's Deputy, which indicates that
Horemheb – being without a son to succeed him – had nominated Ramesses
his heir. Ramesses came from a comparatively obscure military family in the
north-eastern part of the Delta. That the kingship should pass in this way to
a man of high ability who was not royal indicates an apparent flaw in the
doctrine about succession. If the king had no son and there was no royal
heiress through whom the divine kingship could be transmitted, there was no
alternative to the arrangement that led to the elevation of Ramesses I. Because
Amon had, as an oracle, been invited to make the decision, it would not have
been regarded as an arrangement. A king, it seems, could be king by birth,
by marriage, or by divine intervention; and, of course, ideally by all three.

For the ancients nothing happened that was entirely arbitrary, or brought
about by chance or luck. Everything was intended by supernatural forces.
Not only the ancients thought in this way. When Charles Darwin's *Origin of
Species* met with hostility, it was because orthodox religion in the nineteenth
century took the view that nothing happened by the mindless elimination of
the less successful but only by the will of God. For the Ancient Egyptians the
legitimacy of a man's claim to the throne was an issue almost as important to
them as evolution was to the Victorians, and they would have found it incon-
ceivable that the king could be named by anyone but the gods and, at the time
of the empire, more particularly by Amon-Re. When he came to the throne
by divine election Ramesses I was already elderly and reigned only a very short
time, to be succeeded by his more famous son, Seti. As might be expected of a
new dynasty who were aware their legitimacy might still be secretly questioned, they were strongly conservative in their policies. They rebuilt and
added to the traditional cult centres at Thebes and elsewhere. They presented

*Previous page : Ramesses II symbolically offering foreign prisoners to
Amon-Re. Here he is holding an Asiatic, a Nubian, and a Libyan by the hair*

Ramesses II and one of his sons offering geese to Amon and Mut.
Ramesses pulls the barque of the god Soqaris towards his father Seti I

themselves as the legitimate successors to the Tuthmosids and ignored their Amarna predecessors, Akhenaten, Smenkhkare, Tutankhamon, and Ay, not so much out of any detestation of Akhenaten as out of a wish to establish continuity with the great imperial achievements of the past. The real execration of Akhenaten came later. Seti I was not only an energetic soldier, he was a pious respecter of tradition and built elaborately at Abydos where the very earliest kings of Egypt had been buried. One of the ancient tombs was taken to be that of Osiris himself. At the very least his head was buried there, or so it was supposed.

Seti I would have had a particular interest in Osiris because he was named after Set, who murdered him, cut his body up, and distributed the parts throughout Egypt. Who Osiris originally was no one really knows. Oddly enough the ceremonial beard worn by pharaohs and certain gods may provide a clue. There is no obvious reason why Egyptians should wear false beards. They did not grow much hair on the face – that was a characteristic of unclean Asiatics, who are usually shown with beards on tomb and temple walls. A closer look at pharaoh's artificial beard reveals, however, that it is no imitation of a foreign style nor of any beard actually grown by a human in the Nile valley. It grows from the point of the chin, is quite long and looks less like a man's beard than an animal's – a goat, in fact. If so, he relates to a very ancient god indeed who was perhaps to be identified with Osiris, a goat-god before he migrated from the Delta where his home was to Abydos where he became a man with crook and flail and god of the underworld.

Whoever he might have been, the story has it that his own brother Set murdered him. The dismembered Osiris was put together again by his wife Isis, a kind of resurrection was achieved, and their son, Horus, was eventually victorious over Set. Every pharaoh, including Seti I, was thought to be Horus incarnate and he had a special Horus name. Because of the significance of his names Seti may have considered himself a reconciler and a celebrator of national unity. The great temple that he built at Abydos – the oldest major building surviving at this most holy of sites – was a national shrine with seven chapels side by side, to Re-Harakhte, Ptah, Amon, Osiris, Isis, Horus, and to Seti himself. Out of deference to the special significance of the site Set was given no place among the divine occupants and his ideogram was not even used in the writing of Seti's cartouche as it should have been; Osiris was substituted.

In compiling his king-lists Manetho would presumably have consulted the genealogical gallery built by Seti in his temple at Abydos; here in the wall reliefs we can see the king and his young son Ramesses (later Ramesses II) burning incense and reciting hymns in front of the names of seventy-six wearers of the double crown from Menes onwards, but excluding the Amarna pharaohs. What was not mentioned did not exist, what was erased was consigned to oblivion, but what was represented in word or picture potentially – so the theory went – could last for ever. The very many statues and temples of some pharaohs, notably Ramesses II, may owe their existence to the hope that at least one of them would survive through all eternity.

Such was Seti's piety, a temple was not enough. Seti I's tomb is the most magnificent in the Valley of the Kings, its passages and chambers extending for some hundred metres, but to preserve his presence at Abydos he built a cenotaph there. This is a curious structure immediately west of the main temple. He gave instructions to dig down to the water table and in the pool then formed to build a rectangular island to represent the primal mound that

The mummy cover of Ramesses II from the Cairo Museum

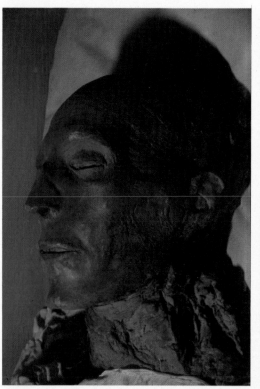

emerged from chaos on the first day of creation, rather as islands appeared when the annual Nile inundation began to recede. On the island were placed a sarcophagus and a canopic chest – the receptacle, that is to say, for jars containing the viscera of the dead. Around the moat were many niches, presumably where gods were represented. Beyond the central tomb area were transverse chambers, in one of which a replica of Seti's catafalque was intended to rest. The walls of the entrance to the cenotaph were decorated with scenes from the traditional books about the after-life – the Book of Gates, the Book of the Dead, the Book of Caverns – and elsewhere were illustrations to do with traditional cosmology. All this was given a roof supported in part by ten pink granite pillars. When Strabo, the Greek geographer, visited the site in 25 BC he spoke of gaining access to the 'palace' by passages with low vaults. It put him in mind of the famous Twelfth Dynasty labyrinth in the Fayoum. The cenotaph was a calculated mystery, dimly lit, if at all, by natural means but more likely illuminated by oil lamps to symbolize the lamp-lit search made through the night by Isis for the body of Osiris.

The cenotaph of Seti I was something of a political statement. In the temple he had established his lineage as pharaoh. Here, in the darkness, he was identifying himself with the most ancient rituals and beliefs of Egypt. Set was as old as Osiris; originally a storm-god, he was now a god of deserts and foreigners, a most worthy deity in the king's eyes, but he had killed his brother. 'I,' Seti seems to claim in his cenotaph, 'acknowledge the powers of darkness as well as the powers of light. I am the seed growing again after the harvest has been gathered, I am the victim and his murderer, I am the reconciler of all contradictions.' He provided his dynasty with a considered and no doubt deeply considered attitude to its cultural inheritance and a base from which to launch the initiatives the new age seemed to call for. He spoke of his reign quite literally as a renaissance, a repeating of births, a time when the greatness of the past would be made to live again.

Judging a man's character from his face is questionable at the best of times but to judge it from his mummified face is probably to deceive ourselves. Seti's mummy, though, is unusually well preserved. He was a handsome man with a firm, almost peaked jaw and an expression that could verge on the genial. For all his apparent amiability, his veneration for the past was such that he revived the practice of clubbing rebellious vassals to death before Amon. He was, in fact, a tough disciplinarian. He published a decree to protect the privileges of his Abydos foundation which resembles Horemheb's in the severity of the punishments; a steward of the temple's cattle who mis-

The mummies of many New Kingdom pharaohs were unexpectedly discovered in 1881. Among them were Seti I (above left); Ramesses II (above right); and Seqenenre (below), whose shattered skull shows that he was probably killed fighting the Hyksos

Seti I charging the Libyans in his chariot brandishing a sickle sword

appropriated them would be impaled on a stake, his wife and children forfeit to the Chief Priest of the temple, and the cattle returned a hundredfold. Rustlers were to have their ears and noses cut off. In truth, it sounds a bit unrealistic but the decree does provide evidence that Seti believed in cracking the whip. (One wonders, incidentally, why this decree was published on a stela six hundred miles to the south, just north of the Third Cataract. Perhaps there were other versions in different parts of his dominions and the decree did not mean precisely what it said but was a public flexing of pharaoh's muscles.)

It would be naïve to assume that a pharaoh's lapidary inscriptions are to be taken at their face value. One of Seti's stelae on the desert road some miles east of Edfu does, however, seem to strike a genuinely personal note. This was the road that led to the gold-fields near the Red Sea and Seti had apparently travelled this road in person. 'Woe to the man thirsty in this wilderness,' he said. He had a well dug and a settlement founded with the idea of providing better facilities for travellers, particularly those bringing the gold-dust back to Abydos and the gold-washers themselves who, Seti hoped, 'would bless my name in years to come . . . inasmuch as I am compassionate and regardful of travellers'.

He was the first pharaoh for nearly 150 years to leave clear evidence of trying to repeat the successes of Tuthmosis III in Palestine and Syria. In the first year of his reign Seti I embarked on a campaign across Sinai. The army was embarked at Memphis but did not follow Tuthmosis III's example of sailing all the way to Syria. It disembarked at Tjel at the eastern end of the military road across Sinai, the Horus Road, 120 miles long, and then marched, as Amosis had marched, behind a chariot bearing a pole on the top of which was the ram's head of Amon and, only a little below that, a statuette of pharaoh himself.

The extent to which Egyptian communications were threatened is shown by the fact that Seti had to fight even in Sinai. At intervals along the military road were wells, each protected by a *migdol* fortress and its garrison of Egyptian soldiers. Seti found some of these *migdol* fortresses under siege from Beduin tribesmen who had to be driven off before marching on to the fortified city of Gaza, once an Egyptian stronghold, but which now had to be taken by storm. Seti's strength must have been overwhelming because, pausing only to pick up scared Canaanites hiding in the bushes, he was soon beyond Megiddo, which had been held all the time by its Egyptian garrison, to relieve the siege of Beth-shan, south of Lake Galilee, where an Egyptian force had been under attack from the local princelings. North Palestine, out to Pella in the east and to Acre in the west, was rapidly traversed by various sections of Seti's army before he struck north into Lebanon, where he exacted a tribute of timber before returning in triumph to Egypt. The impression given is that pharaoh's control of territory in Palestine and Syria was spotty.

The following year he penetrated even further north to the traditional focus of military resistance to the Egyptians, Kadesh – that fortified city on its hill with castellated walls and a huge gateway, all behind two moats fed by water from the Orontes. It was the key to northern Syria and somewhere hereabouts on his fourth and last campaign Seti fought a battle with the Hittites under their king Murshil which in Egypt was claimed as a victory. Seti's line of communications was too extended and too much under threat for him to sustain the kind of pressure on the Hittites that would have given the Egyptians a real hold on northern Syria, and a peace treaty was concluded which recognized that an effective boundary between the two powers ran somewhere south of Kadesh. The whole area was still unstable politically because of the military stalemate but Seti had certainly made it clear that a revival of Egyptian power in the area was under way. Egypt probably had as much power in Syria at this time as even under Tuthmosis III. What had been lost since the time of Amenophis III had been made good.

Seti's son Ramesses was an exuberant young man who thought he lived in the morning of the world and could do even better than his father. His is the most famous name in Ancient Egyptian history. He reigned so long, at least sixty-seven years, and such glories were attributed to him that for generations after he was dead pharaohs called themselves Ramesses as though by doing so they could revive the past. He is Ozymandias and came to personify the splendours of empire in a way no other pharaoh did. Because of the scale of his building he makes his presence felt even today.

Ramesses II was in his late teens when his father died in 1304 BC. The court was normally resident at Memphis but Thebes was the religious capital and one of Ramesses' first recorded acts was to travel there for the Feast of Opet. Anything less than the king's presence when Amon-Re emerged from his sanctuary and sailed south to Luxor for the first time during his reign would have been badly received in Thebes, particularly as the office of Chief Priest appeared to be vacant. Only the king could consult the divine oracle on such an important matter as the succession. He placed the names of candidates before the shrine, supported by bearers, and the shrine then signified 'with a great nod' that the chosen one was a certain Nebunenef who happened to be High Priest of Osiris at Abydos. On his way back to Memphis Ramesses accordingly stopped at Abydos to confirm Nebunenef in his new office and to inspect the as yet unfinished temple which his father had started. In the presence of the assembled court he declared his intention of completing it. Towards the end of his father's life the administration of his temple had been neglected, the offerings had ceased, and the lay priests become lax in their service – rather a surprising falling off when one remembers the rigorous terms of Seti's decree. Ramesses was now going to see that the temple endowments were restored and, by making new appointments, ensure the foundation's permanent well-being. Perhaps Nebunenef, previously Chief Priest at various southern temples, had succeeded in calling favourable attention to himself by complaining about the unsatisfactory state of affairs at Abydos.

The first Syrian campaign was not launched until the fourth year of

A detail from the Ramesseum showing Hittite chariotry (above) with their three-man crew. The lighter Egyptians (opposite above) fought with two men. The Sherden (opposite below) with their round shields and horned helmets were usually prisoners conscripted into the Egyptian army

Ramesses' reign and his inscription near the mouth of the Dog River, un-decipherable but for the date, is there to this day, together with inscriptions made by other Egyptian, Asiatic, and European armies over the centuries. Palestine and southern Lebanon were securely in his hands and the following year Ramesses decided on a major campaign against the Hittites. He was plainly the aggressor. The attack was in breach of solemn agreements about spheres of influence but Ramesses plainly wanted to do better even than his father and break through to the riches of northern Syria which the king of the Hittites, now Mutawallish, regarded as his territory. King Mutawallish was at the head of a confederacy covering most of Anatolia and parts of Upper Mesopotamia. The army of about seventeen thousand men which he gathered to resist Ramesses included contingents from as far away as Troy and the Aegean. Mitanni, no longer an independent force, was a leading state in this confederacy and was strongly represented, together with the other senior member, Arzawa, inland from present-day Smyrna. Mutawallish's hetero-geneous army was strong in chariotry, still the chief Asiatic assault weapon though used in rather a different way from the Egyptians.

The Hittite chariot transported three men, a driver, a shield bearer, and a warrior armed with a spear or javelin. It seems to have been thought of as a moveable platform for transporting troops as rapidly as the rough ground permitted into the ranks of the enemy who were then engaged in hand-to-hand fighting. This meant they could move superior manpower very rapidly into battle areas where it counted most. The Egyptians, on the other hand, had only two men in their chariots, a charioteer and a bowman. Tactics varied, no doubt, from battle to battle but the characteristic Egyptian assault was by chariotry which, at the appropriate distance from the enemy lines, would wheel so that the bowman could use his powerful composite bow in the hope of transfixing as many of the enemy as possible, rather as Amenophis II had delighted to hit copper targets while being driven at full gallop. Egyptian chariots had runners as well, armed men who did their best to keep up with the horses and, after the shock inflicted on the enemy by the barrage of arrows, would be ready to charge into the demoralized ranks of the enemy with their spears and axes.

We know a great deal about this Syrian campaign of Ramesses II because he had it represented on temple walls from one end of Egypt to the other. He took four divisions, each made up of chariotry, archers, and infantry to a strength of five thousand men, leading the premier division of Amon him-self. For the first time there is mention of a Ptah division. The other two were the divisions of Re and Setekh. The great majority of these troops were Egyptian; among the bowmen there was a preponderance of Nubians. Under Ramesses contingents of foreign soldiers were for the first time incorporated in the army. To describe them as mercenaries is inaccurate because they were Libyan and Sherden prisoners who were given no alternative to military service. For years the Sherden had been coming across the Mediterranean from some unknown country of origin to make piratical raids into the Delta; they are the same people who some considerable time later went west and gave their name to the island of Sardinia. The Sherden conscripts in the army that Ramesses II took into Syria in 1300 BC, with their short swords and strange horned helmets, could not have been entirely reliable particularly if, as was not impossible, they came up against their own kin in the Hittite army. Camping equipment, cooking utensils, spare parts for chariots, the golden throne of pharaoh, and gods in their portable shrines were transported in ox-drawn waggons, on the backs of donkeys and mules, or even in chariots that were sometimes used for moving goods.

Reaching Lebanon, Ramesses sent off a task force to follow the coast road and seize a port, probably Sumura, so that the Egyptian navy could sail in and ensure quick sea communication with the Delta. Ramesses led the main army inland to the Beka'a plain on the other side of the Lebanon range and then north to the valley of the Orontes where Kadesh barred the way. Egyptians were accustomed to planning by the calendar and there is no reason to doubt that their military campaigns were to a carefully considered timetable. The Sumura task force, Ramesses must have calculated, would complete its mission and be in time to join him at Kadesh for the crucial battle.

But a characteristic of all Egyptian commanders, Tuthmosis III not excepted, was impetuosity. Even allowing for pharaoh's repeated wish to claim that he had behaved heroically in difficult circumstances – exaggerating and even inventing the dangers – royal commanders-in-chief do seem to have exposed themselves unnecessarily. The wonder is that none of the warrior pharaohs, with the possible exception of Seqenenre, was ever ambushed. Ramesses II, as he approached Kadesh, showed surprising lack of prudence and even gullibility.

He caused the Amon division to ford the Orontes in early morning at Shabtuna, which is about twenty kilometres up stream from Kadesh itself, and enter the wood of Robaui where earlier campaigning pharaohs had hunted for pleasure. This was precisely the sort of terrain where an ambush might be expected. The marching Nubians and Egyptians of the Amon division, their legs still numb from wading through the icy water, would be keeping a tight grip on their spears. The strangeness of forest and rushing water made them uneasy. The glistening flanks of the horses gave off vapour in the rising sun, the chariot wheels cut so deep into the marshy ground that the charioteers, even the king himself, got out and walked to reduce the load. Voices were kept low. Ramesses climbed on to a rock where he could stand in the full sun to watch the division pass and provide the boost to morale that the undoubted splendour of his appearance, in blue Atef crown and bronze corselet, the living Horus, would work on the men. He was waiting to learn just where the Hittite army was, for his scouts had so far failed to locate it.

It was now, however, that the scouts picked up two local men, Shasu, who said they wanted to come over and serve pharaoh. As for the Hittite army, that was nowhere near Kadesh but many miles away to the north at Aleppo. These two men were Hittite agents sent by Mutawallish to give false information designed to lead Ramesses into a trap, which is more or less what happened. Believing what he wanted to believe, Ramesses swallowed the story that Kadesh was his for the taking and pressed on at the head of the Amon division, not even waiting for the rest of the army. No doubt this was to the apprehension of his commanders. There is no mention of a camp council in the Egyptian records at this juncture, doubtless because Ramesses overruled his senior officers and led them to near disaster. No faking of the evidence could have obscured this because it would have necessitated Ramesses saying that the rapid advance he now ordered was against his better judgement; no pharaoh could make such an admission.

The Amon division marched on through the wood and camped to the west of Kadesh in the traditional rectangular compound protected by a fence of shields, not unlike the Roman military camp of more than a thousand years later. The scene was an immensely active one – horses, donkeys, and oxen being watered, chariots repaired, food distributed and pharaoh's tent being set up with his pet lion tethered to a post and looking on. In the middle of all this banging of hammers two more Hittite agents were brought in, having been found skulking among the trees. After a severe beating they revealed the true whereabouts of Mutawallish's army. It was gathered in strength on the eastern side of Kadesh and consisted of about 17,000 men, with 2500 chariots. The make-up of the Hittite army was therefore about 10,000 infantry and, allowing three men to a chariot, 7500 in the chariotry. It could not be seen by Ramesses' scouts because the hill and fortifications of Kadesh were in the way.

Ramesses immediately realized he was in danger of having to fight the battle of Megiddo all over again, with the Egyptian and enemy roles reversed. In that battle the Egyptians had been able to attack while the Syrians were regrouping. And now the Hittites would attack while the Amon division was in camp and the three other divisions were still on the march. The rear-most division, that of Setekh, had not even forded the river on the other side of the wood of Robaui. The only advantage Ramesses possessed, and of which he hoped the Hittites knew nothing, was the existence of the task force he had sent up the coast of Sumura and could be expected to join the main army at

The battle of Kadesh as shown on the walls of the Ramesseum. The fortified city of Kadesh, protected by the Orontes, is at the right with Hittite troops drawn up below it. Ramesses II is charging them in his chariot from the top left

any moment. After an urgent camp council he sent a messenger and then the Vizier himself to warn the Re division and order a more rapid march to join him.

Just as the Re division was emerging from the wood of Robaui, some eight kilometres south of Ramesses' camp, it was attacked by the Hittites while still in column of route. Before the Egyptians could understand what was happening, the Hittite chariots cut through them and men were speared down before they could draw their bows. The survivors fled, some back into the wood, some into the hills to the west but most to the north where the Hittites now chased them into the Amon camp.

The Egyptian intelligence service must have broken down in the confusion; Ramesses and the Amon division seem to have been completely taken by surprise. The various Egyptian reliefs showing the battle indicate that while the Hittites were breaking through the palisade at one end of the camp, the Egyptians at the other end were mainly occupied watering their horses, mending bows and other equipment. But it was a convention of Egyptian art that events taking place at different times could be shown as though simultaneous. In fact the Hittites were no sooner inside the camp defences than most of the Amon division took to its heels, leaving Ramesses and a chariot force of indeterminate size behind. Ramesses subsequently told the story rather differently. He claimed to have been completely deserted, but this is well within the established tradition that pharaohs claimed where possible the sole credit for military feats. The reason he was not chopped down soon after noon one spring day over three thousand years ago was due almost certainly to his own valour. No one has ever doubted that Ramesses was a courageous soldier. He would have shouted, 'Great Amon, consider what I have done for you. Now do a little thing for me.' And he would have rallied his chariotry and made a counter-attack.

What chiefly saved him was the way Hittite discipline broke down, as Egyptian discipline had broken down at Megiddo. In these otherwise tightly controlled ancient armies discipline usually did break down when there was booty for the taking. Instead of getting on with the fighting the Hittites began plundering the camp. In answer to Ramesses' prayer to Amon the task force from the coast now arrived and attacked the Hittites when they least expected it. Although Mutawallish brought up reinforcements, the Egyptians were

Opposite above : The most impressive of Ramesses II's monuments is the rock temple of Abu Simbel in Nubia
Opposite below : His funerary temple, the Ramesseum on the west bank of Thebes, was on a gigantic scale. The fallen colossus shown here remotely inspired Shelley's Ozymandias
Overleaf : Ramesses II as he wished his subjects to see him, overcoming the Hittites

now able to rally sufficiently for the launching of a number of chariot charges which were not of the usual kind but straight into the enemy ranks. In the confused hand-to-hand fighting that resulted a man had difficulty in knowing friend from foe. The Egyptian counter-offensive saved the day for Ramesses and before night fell the van of the newly arrived Ptah division was able to join in driving the Hittites back into the Orontes, where the prince of Aleppo swallowed so much water that he had to be held upside down by his soldiers for it to pour out. The Setekh division was still in the wood of Robaui and took no part in the fighting.

A resolute commander might, after a night's rest, have re-engaged the Hittites but Ramesses decided he lacked the resources to press any advantage he may have possessed. For their part Mutawallish's forces had taken a mauling and one Egyptian account of the battle says that the next day he asked for a truce or armistice. If so it gave the Egyptians no advantage and certainly conceded no defeat. But there was no more fighting.

The Hittite version of the battle, which was discovered only comparatively recently in the remains of the archives at Hattushash, says that it was a defeat for Ramesses and that he had to retreat, giving up territory and pretensions in northern Syria that his father Seti I had claimed. The Hittite version is nearer the truth than Ramesses' contention that he had won a decisive and single-handed victory at Kadesh. The claim was repeated in the Kadesh reliefs with which he delighted to decorate his temples in Karnak, Luxor, Abu Simbel, in his funerary temple, the Ramesseum, and elsewhere. No doubt he had been personally brave after his initial tactical blunder and he had been lucky. Even if he had known the task force from the coast was so near when he marched the division of Amon up from the wood of Robaui to Kadesh, he could not have foreseen how truly providential that nearness was to be. It would not be correct to say that Ramesses was defeated at Kadesh but he certainly had a set-back. He marched his depleted army south and Mutawallish followed him as far as Damascus, which Ramesses must have resented a great deal; Damascus was well within recognized Egyptian territory. As the remnants of the Amon division tramped through Palestine, with their ox-carts transporting dead officers of enough seniority to be preserved in natron, their demoralization would not have been helped by such open mockery from the locals as was dared. (Egyptians attached such importance to burial in Egypt one surmises that natron waggons travelled with the army and paradoxically were quite a factor in maintaining morale. Ordinary soldiers had no expectation higher than a local, shallow grave.)

In later years Ramesses campaigned repeatedly in Syria. As he raided into Hittite territory beyond Kadesh as far as Tunip and Qatna, it must have

Opposite : Within the rock temple of Abu Simbel, Ramesses II is repeatedly represented in giant statues

159

seemed the great days had come again. At Qatna his military intelligence was defective once more; there was a Hittite attack that took him so much by surprise he went into battle without his coat of mail. In the long run he was not capable, though, of the sustained military effort needed to pin the Hittites back. Even in Palestine he had to deal with revolts as far south as Ashkelon. From the Western Desert there was a different kind of threat. It came from the various Libyan peoples who wanted to move east into the Delta and settle there. From his father's time there had been fighting to keep these Libyans out and Ramesses built a string of forts from Rhakotis, on the present site of Alexandria to the west of El Alamein, controlling the invasion route into Egypt and frustrating as much as possible the dangerous alliance that was growing up between the Libyans and the Sherden raiders. But if Ramesses could not bring off a conclusive victory over the Hittites, they, for their part, could not aspire to any control south of Kadesh; for them there were other dangers nearer at hand, from Assyria in particular. The two great states had an interest in calling a halt to their rivalry and this, when Ramesses was still not yet forty years old, is what they did in 1284 BC, sixteen years after the battle of Kadesh. By this time the Hittite king was Khattushilish.

A peace treaty inscribed on silver tablets was concluded as between two equal powers, in which they declared they would not go to war again. A frontier between the two empires was agreed though oddly enough its precise position was not stated; it probably ran south of Kadesh and Amurru. If support was needed by either against any third power it would be given. What is more Egypt and Khatti were to support each other in asserting their authority over their respective spheres of influence. The hard fact was that Ramesses gave up traditional claims to northern Syria. Talk of an empire that stretched to the banks of the Euphrates was no longer possible.

There were many earlier treaties between states in the Ancient East but this is the oldest of which there is a full record. The remarkable fact is that the text is available both in Egyptian hieroglyphs (on a stela at Karnak) and in a cuneiform version found at Hattushash. An interesting detail into which the treaty goes is the treatment of fugitives. One of the running irritants of the day was the manner in which political or criminal fugitives could take sanctuary across state frontiers. Ramesses and Khattushilish now agreed extradition clauses which were intended to have the effect, presumably, of damping down sedition and crime. But in fact the terms of the agreement make it clear that the returned offender was not to be punished, nor were his wife and children to suffer. A murderer, say, who had bolted from an Egyptian stronghold in Galilee to Aleppo and was then returned under the extradition agreement seemed entitled to a pardon. Perhaps the fugitive was regarded in the host country as having a special claim on its honour and hospitality. Handing him back to his native state could be done, then, as a courtesy but immunity from punishment was required to show that no man could appeal in vain to the king of Khatti or pharaoh for sanctuary. The question was one not so much of justice to the individual as of a proper regard for the dignity of independent and equal great rulers. But all this applied to men of low rank. For 'great men' who were fugitives for political reasons, there was no saving clause in the extradition agreement; they were simply returned to wherever they came from and were presumably then tried and punished according to the law of their native land.

The peace this treaty inaugurated was lasting. Eighty-four years after it was signed, in 1200 BC, the Hittite empire was destroyed by a combination of dissident vassals and fighting people who migrated into the area from western Anatolia and the Aegean and who were known to the Egyptians themselves as 'Peoples of the Sea'. During those eighty-four years relations between Egypt and Khatti were cordial, remarkably so in some respects. Thirteen years after the treaty Ramesses married Khattushilish's eldest daughter, who took the Egyptian name of Matnefrure. To Ramesses' surprise she made the journey in winter when heavy rain and floods could so easily render the roads

The southern gate of the Hittite capital of Hattushash

impassable. He made an offering to Set, the god with a special responsibility for foreign countries, to ensure good weather. Even at normal times Ramesses enjoyed widely recognized powers of controlling the rain in Asia, to the extent of withholding it at seed time from nations he wished to punish. On this auspicious occasion the combined powers of Set and Ramesses were responsible for exceptionally mild weather and the princess arrived safely at the head of a force of Hittite soldiers. At the frontier in Palestine the troops of Egypt 'mingled with the foot and horse of the Hittites' and there was fraternizing between the ancient enemies in an atmosphere of high festival. Ramesses received the princess at the new capital he had built in the north-east Delta, Per-Ramesse as it was called. Khattushilish himself does not appear to have come – though a later visit is rumoured – but it was marvel enough that Hittite captains could stand in pharaoh's audience chamber and then take part in the state banquet with perfumed oil upon their heads.

The god Ptah of Memphis said it was he, out of regard for his son Ramesses, who had made this unprecedented new relationship with the Hittites possible. Ramesses responded by enlarging the temple of Ptah at Memphis, endowing it with 'priests, prophets, slaves, land and cattle beyond limit' and eventually publishing the facts in his new temple cut into the rock cliff overlooking the Nile at Abu Simbel in Nubia.

Looked at from the point of view of the vassal states of Syria and Palestine the treaty gave promise of much needed stability. The buffer state of Amurru which had been claimed as a client by both Egypt and the Hittites was now firmly in the Hittite fold and no Egyptian army would march in again to storm the fortified cities of Tunip and Qatna; no prince of Amurru would attack Byblos in the way reported by Rib-Addi in the time of Akhenaten. In Egypt itself peace led to prosperity. From the point of view of the rising power of Assyria, however, the treaty was a set-back. The king of Assyria had recently claimed the title of 'Great King' – a designation to put him on equal terms with any other monarch of the day – and had been rebuked for his pretensions by Khattushilish who said bluntly in a letter that has survived, 'Don't write about Great Kingship to me.'

Ramesses professed to be quite delighted with the new order he and Khattushilish had established, though he never ceased from representing himself as the conqueror of the Hittites. Between Hattushash and Per-Ramesse there was a flow of ambassadors, messengers, and trading missions. Pharaoh wrote to the Great King and the Great King wrote to pharaoh. Queen Nefertari, Ramesses' Great Wife, wrote to Pudu-Kheba, queen of the Hittites, who then wrote back. The extraordinary thing about this correspondence is that the letters written by Ramesses and Nefertari were always identical, and so were the letters they received in reply. Nothing quite like this duplicated correspondence is known from any other time and if it implies any kind of feminine ascendancy it does not seem to have interfered with a second marriage by Ramesses to a Hittite princess. According to a much later tradition Ramesses heard that a younger sister of his Hittite wife Matnefrure was ill; he sent first of all a physician and, when his efforts proved in vain, a miracle-working statue of the god Khonsu, rather as Ishtar of Nineveh had been sent to cure Amenophis III's toothache. This is not a historical record but it would be true to the spirit of the times if Khonsu brought the cured younger sister of Matnefrure back to Per-Ramesse where she became yet another of his many queens.

Ramesses fathered over 150 children, was enormously proud of the fact, and lived so long that many of them died before he did. One daughter married a Syrian sea captain so he may have had difficulty in finding suitable husbands for all the girls. He built more temples and had himself represented in more colossal statues than any other pharaoh. He usurped the monuments of his predecessors, even his own father's, and destroyed ancient temples for raw material to use in his own new buildings. He built a great new city. His inscribed utterances are so bombastic that he is sometimes dismissed as a self-glorifying megalomaniac but this is a modern reaction and not how he was thought of in the ancient world. No less than nine pharaohs after him were so anxious to inherit something of his splendour that they chose to be called Ramesses too. His grandiloquence was in a well-worn tradition. The taste for the grandiose was nothing new. The enormous hypostyle hall at Karnak which Ramesses completed and which is often thought of as the supreme expression in stone of the achievements of his reign was in fact started by Amenophis III. Even so, Ramesses was a compulsive builder of the colossal and one wonders whether, deep down, it indicated a basic uncertainty about any values, even the central authority of pharaoh.

His narrow escape at Kadesh marked him. The sight of Hittite warriors breaking through the palisade of his camp and being cut down by his guards no more than fifty metres from where he was standing would have shaken most commanders. The success of his counter-attacks must have seemed a clear sign of divine intervention on his behalf; so, in the most unmistakable way, he would have known he was specially favoured by the gods. If he ever woke in a sweat because of a bad dream it would be one of ambush yet, wide awake, he would know the fear of ambush was only sent by some hostile spirit. In reality he had nothing to fear. He was a god himself and in the care of the gods. He was like Montu, the god of war himself. The sun-god, his father, loved him. He and Montu would stand at his either hand ready to shout down any hostile spirit that came in the night. The place where fears and uncertainties could genuinely be resolved was on the battlefield. But now that major campaigning was a thing of the past, the only way Ramesses seemingly could come to terms with himself and his unquenchable vitality was through endless building and the raising of multitudinous statues of himself in compulsive, magical reiteration. If not fighting what else could a pharaoh do?

Artistically, Ramesses was not sensitive but he plainly loved the mechanics of quarrying huge pieces of stone, transporting them on sledges and barges, and the complicated but ancient techniques of carving, chiselling, polishing, and, above all, manoeuvring them into place. In the quarries of the Red Mountain not far from Heliopolis he personally identified a block of stone suitable for sculpting into a colossal representation of himself; and he set up a stela to record the way he looked after the interests of the quarrymen and stone carvers; he gave them wheat, meat, clothes, and sandals with 'perfumes to anoint your heads every ten days'. (The rest day was every tenth in Ancient Egypt.) He built temples everywhere but probably none gave him greater satisfaction than the Nubian temples cut out of the rock at Abu Simbel. The engineering difficulties were considerable. Because of the narrowness of the cultivable strip of land at this point, work had already started during his father's reign on cutting into the cliff face. The four colossal statues of Ramesses, the façade and the interior chambers were 'hewn in the pure mountain' to a depth of sixty metres for the main temple, so aligned that in winter the rays struck through the length of the temple to the sanctuary and illuminated the four gods, Amon-Re, Re-Harakhte, Ptah, and Ramesses himself. The alignment of this temple and that of the smaller one to the north in honour of the king's Great Wife, Nefertari, have been preserved in the new position on top of the cliff where they were moved to avoid being engulfed by the waters of the new High Dam. It was a prodigious engineering feat entirely in the Ramesside tradition.

He was much taken by foreign gods and manners. In the epic poem written to commemorate his exploits at Kadesh and inscribed on the temple walls of Karnak, Luxor, and Abydos, he is at one point compared not to the usual Egyptian gods but to the Semitic god Baal of Canaan. At Per-Ramesse he built a temple to the Syrian goddess Anat, after whom he named not only his mares but his favourite daughter, Bint-Anat. He lavished his favours on many cults but with such generosity the priests of Amon-Re, Ptah or Re-Harakhte may have recognized there was enough for everyone. Amon-Re still came in for special consideration. In spite of Ramesses spending most of his time in the Delta, Amon-Re of Thebes remained at the centre of priestly power, consolidating his ascendancy as the years went by, perhaps out of some sense in pharaoh of his need to compensate for his absence by even greater gifts of treasure and land; and by prodigious temple building. The great columned hall of the Temple of Amon was his work in the main and it has been variously described as a wonder of Egyptian architecture, as providing a great emotional experience, as being a calculated demonstration of mind-crushing power, and at the same time as being structurally unsound – a surprising statement to make about the largest basilica ever constructed which is still substantially intact after three thousand years and more. The 134 columns, simulating the stems and crowning bud or flower of the papyrus, are enormous, like the gnarled shafts of ancient space rockets arranged on some unbelievable launching pad for simultaneous blast-off. The columns with the open-flowered capitals form a higher central aisle with clerestory windows on the north and south to admit at a height of fifty feet or more the only natural light this high-roofed, echoing audience chamber of the god received. Wherever one looked – and wherever one looks today – diagonally across the hall the pillars close up and block the sight-lines with what looks like a solid stack of gods, kings, and hieroglyphs marching endlessly.

Ramesses not only built great temples himself, like the one near his father's at Abydos and the vanished temples of Per-Ramesse and Memphis which must have been on a comparable scale, he added to earlier temples in a way that sometimes diminished their effect. Hence the charge of insensitivity. Amenophis III's temple at Luxor was given an unnecessary courtyard and new monumental entrance with six more colossal statues of himself plus two red granite obelisks in a way that implies he was claiming the achievement of the whole temple complex for himself. To make this possible he, or his architect, the Chief Priest of Amon, Bekenkhonsu, destroyed a fine granite chapel of Tuthmosis III's which, had we the choice, would be preferable to what is in its place. Bekenkhonsu, incidentally, was the same age as Ramesses when this work was done and lived nearly as long.

On the other side of the Nile his funerary temple, the Ramesseum, with its three hypostyle halls and two huge courtyards was a considered record of the king's life and ambitions. Here on the honey-coloured walls are the accounts of his Syrian campaigns and here, too, is the fallen and shattered colossus that must originally have weighed a thousand tons and was commemorated by Shelley in his poem 'Ozymandias'. Ramesses' building programme was so over-ambitious as to be absurd. One question to which there can be no answer is whether he cultivated his building obsession as a way of not thinking about the real and insoluble problems he was vaguely aware existed but could not quite get into focus. Were there gods he did not know about? What could he do now that would ensure there was no falling away by his people when he was dead?

He would have remembered that bright morning in the very first year of his reign when he had disembarked at Abydos and told Nebunenef that he was to be Chief Priest of Amon at Thebes. Even at that early date he had been clear that the priestly function was not to be combined with other great appointments of state. A Chief Priest was a Chief Priest and no more. He was not, as he had been in earlier reigns, Vizier as well, or Chancellor, or Overseer of this or that. A Chief Priest should not have great power outside the spiritual hierarchy. Even Nebunenef's successor, the long-lived and highly esteemed Bekenkhonsu, had not, by Ramesses, been given any of the great state functions nor any special palace status. His official title was Chief Prophet of all the Gods and this, Ramesses would have remembered, was by design. He had wanted to avoid any reference to Upper and Lower Egypt which had been designated the territory of earlier pontiffs because pharaoh alone, in the view of Ramesses, was entitled to claim authority in the Two Lands.

Ramesses would then have corrected himself. Under his predecessors there had often been two Viziers, one for Upper and one for Lower Egypt, but he, in his wisdom, had decided on a single Vizier for the Two Lands precisely because of his wish, while paying all honour to Amon-Re, to demonstrate through his single Vizier that there was only one source of authority in the Two Lands and that was he, pharaoh himself. The natural and supernatural worlds so interpenetrated, the profane and the sacred were such a unity, that the full priestly title was now held not by the Chief Priest of Amon but by the Vizier, Neferrenpet, who became Chief Prophet of all the gods of Upper and Lower Egypt and the title passed on to his successor; Ramesses had not been unaware of the part the Amon priesthood could play in eroding the central authority of the state. It is significant that the sons of ruling pharaohs did not become Chief Priests of Amon whereas it was by no means uncommon for them to be Chief Priests of Ptah, as Amenophis II had been while Crown Prince, and as Khaemuast, a son of Ramesses II, was with such distinction that his fame as a sage lasted into Roman times. The Chief Priesthood of Amon-Re was something different. Obscurely, uncertainly, hesitantly it was being seen as an alternative centre of power. This was the kind of problem Ramesses could not get into focus. Ironically, when right at the end of Ramesses' reign the Chief Priest of Amon, Bekenkhonsu, died in his eighties, the equally aged pharaoh inducted a successor who, while accepting he could not look for the Vizierate or the Ministry of Finance, nevertheless was the first to dream of substituting, in Upper Egypt at least, the rule of the Chief Priest for that of the divine king and making the office hereditary. His name was Roma-Roy and his story belongs to a later reign.

For a long time there has been uncertainty where the new city of Per-Ramesse was located. This is the city that according to Exodus 1:12 the Israelites built together with the other 'store city' of Pithom. But Per-Ramesse was very much more than a store city if by that is meant a granary centre. Writers of the time were ecstatic in its praises. Its great buildings were embellished with glazed tiles the colour of turquoise and lapis-lazuli; the river, the lakes, and the canals teemed with fish; vineyards produced wine of Kankeme 'sweeter than honey'; its granaries were full of wheat; all fruits and vegetables grew there in abundance – pomegranates, apples, olives, figs – and whatever the city lacked could be brought by sea-going ships right into the busy harbour.

That Seti I and Ramesses II should make their main base in the north-east Delta is understandable. It was the part of Egypt their family came from;

more important was its position at the centre of communications between
Egypt and Palestine. For the same reason the Hyksos kings had placed their
capital of Avaris on this very site. The remains of their great temple to Set –
or Setekh as they called him – have recently been uncovered in the southern
quarter of the city precisely where the contemporary papyri said it was, with
blue-washed walls and easy access to the almost circular harbour that led off
the Pelusiac branch of the Nile. Ships could sail from here upstream to
Memphis and Thebes, downstream to the Mediterranean and so to Crete,
Cyprus, Palestine, and Syria; or, by canal and lake to Tjel, the penitentiary
settlement which was at the start of the military road through Sinai to Rafia.
To the east of the city were swamps, lakes, creeks, and Yam-suf, the 'Sea of
Reeds', which in the English version of Exodus was mistakenly translated as
the Red Sea.

Only since 1976 when excavations were seriously started by the Austrian
Institute of Archaeology in Cairo at a site known as Tell el-Daba just south of
Qantir has it been firmly established where Avaris and Per-Ramesse were.
The excavations leave no doubt that the site is here, well south of the present
course of the Nile distributory which has shifted its course. One reason why
the site was for so long thought to be further north at Tanis was the number
of the remains there dating from the time of Ramesses II. It is now clear that
they were taken to Tanis at a later date when pharaohs of the Twenty-first
and Twenty-second Dynasties used the Tell el-Daba site as a quarry. Among
the statues, the pillars, and the stelae thus transported was a stela set up by
Ramesses to honour his father, Seti I. The stela tells how Seti, when still a
general and not yet pharaoh, came to Avaris to do honour to the god Set after
whom he was named. This visit, the stela said, was in the four-hundredth
year of the god being established there, a reference now widely understood
to mean that this was the period of time that had elapsed since the Hyksos
built their great temple of Setekh.

If Seti's visit can be placed in the reign of Horemheb, in 1320 BC, as seems
likely, then 1720 BC is the date of the Hyksos first assuming full control of
Avaris. For the establishing of Egyptian chronology this is an important piece
of evidence but what is fascinating about the stela is the way it makes clear
that for Seti and Ramesses the once hated Hyksos no longer had the power to
stir any patriotic passions. They made a clear distinction between the Hyksos
themselves and the cult of Set who, after all, was an Egyptian god long before
the Hyksos were heard of. But it nevertheless seems oddly demonstrative to
make a pilgrimage to Avaris on the four-hundredth anniversary of the setting
up of foreign power there. Since the war of liberation Egypt had been transformed into a cosmopolitan society where Asiatic gods were worshipped and
Canaanite words added to the Egyptian vocabulary. Nationalism was no
more. Old Delta families like the one Ramesses came from may have taken
pride in a more personal link with the past – a tradition, perhaps, of Hyksos

blood in their veins which owed something to the same atavistic promptings that cause an American to talk of his Red Indian ancestry. As can be seen from their mummies, Seti and Ramesses belonged to quite a different physical type from the previous dynasty. Any acknowledgement of an Asiatic root would have pleased the mixed population over which they ruled, particularly in the Delta. For all his bombast Ramesses liked to show he had the human touch. Alone of pharaohs he was regularly referred to during his liketime by a nickname, Sesse.

Our view of Ancient Egypt is very much a pharaoh's-eye view. He recorded the history he wished to be recorded and it is difficult to get behind the official account and establish what ordinary people thought. The state religions were not for them. They were not even allowed into the temples, though a cult of Horus was practised on the outside corner of the temple of Ptah at Memphis. Not inside. The cult of Isis and Osiris is sometimes spoken of as the only truly widespread popular faith because of its emotional content and the promise of eternal life. But there is evidence that men at this time were increasingly turning to religious practices where they felt more involved even than with Osiris. Foreign gods like Astarte, Baal-Sephon, and Anat were brought in by foreign workers and had their following, particularly in Memphis, because a humbler section of the population could gain access to the rites in a way that was not possible in official temples. But these foreign cults stood at an angle to the rest of organized religion in Egypt and did not survive the empire.

There is evidence from Thebes itself of a more personal, confessional religion practised at a level below the official classes. The vast necropolis on the west bank of the Nile at Thebes employed great numbers of artisans and workmen. Their permanent settlement, a village at Deir el-Medina, has been excavated so that it is now possible to walk the streets and enter the living-rooms and workshops of the men who excavated and decorated the rock tombs of Seti I and Ramesses. Here were found memorial stones and stelae carrying hymns and prayers that strike a very different note from temple religion where there was little emphasis on ethical values, and no sense of personal responsibility for one's spiritual well-being or the need for justification. On the Day of Judgement the catechism of the gods could be prepared for like an examination. Virtue could be claimed by going through a whole list of offences and claiming that none had been committed. The gods were remote inquisitors in the state religion but for the Deir el-Medina workmen the gods were not like that. They needed more immediate support and consolation. For the first time in Egypt they gave expression to a personal, con-

Opposite above : The remains of the Funerary Temple of Ramesses II
Opposite below : The workman's village of Deir el-Medina was probably started as early as the time of Amenophis I, but was at its busiest in the time of Ramesses II

fessional faith. A certain draughtsman called Nebre and his son Kha'i put up
a stela in gratitude for the recovery of Nekhtamun, another son, from illness.

> Thou art Amon, Lord of him that is silent:
> Who comest at the voice of this humble man.
> I call upon thee when I am in distress;
> And thou comest that thou mayst save me:
> That Thou mayest give breath to him that is wretched;
> That Thou mayest save me that am in bondage.

There are many others, including prayers for the restoration of sight.
Years of work exposed to rock dust and in bad light, and in a country where
fly-borne eye disease was all too common, led to a lot of blindness. One suppliant asked for mercy of the Peak of the West, which was a particular
eminence above the Theban cliffs associated with a serpent-goddess. Con-
fessing his unworthiness and consciousness of sin the sufferer said he now
saw 'darkness by day'. Deir el-Medina was founded under Queen Ahmose-
Nefertiry and her son Amenophis I so it was natural for them to be at the
centre of strong consolatory cults there. Men could sin but the dead queen
and king were gods who could forgive and sustain.

These prayers may seem ordinary to us but they were unprecedented in
Egypt and seem to indicate a change in the way some men at least perceived
their condition in relation to this world and the next. The change was subtle
and inward. In the settled conditions which Ramesses ruled over for so much
of his long life there is no obvious reason for it. There had been earlier times
in Egyptian history when the evidence is of despair to the point of suicide but
that was due to the general anarchy into which the country had fallen during
the so-called First Intermediate Period between the Middle and New Kingdoms when barons made their own laws. In comparison with that, and what
was to follow, the age of Ramesses the Great was golden. Even so, it is likely
that the personal religion practised in the workmen's village was the result
of some kind of alienation from an increasingly oppressive and impersonal
administration.

Egypt in the Nineteenth Dynasty became a country of functionaries. Control was exerted over every detail of life and to many there seemed no way
bureaucracy could be fought, one's lot improved, or even speaking one's own
mind made possible, as the eloquent peasant in the Middle Kingdom story
had spoken his, saying that eternal life depended on right conduct; and right
conduct was not decided by pharaoh or the Vizier, but was an aspect of the
proper ordering of the universe, *Ma'at*. In the eyes of Ramesses the concept

Opposite : The Beka' a valley looking south towards Mount Hermon.
This is the view which Ramesses II would have seen on his retirement to
Egypt after the battle of Kadesh

of *Ma'at* had been discredited by what Akhenaten had made of it. There was now a tendency to say that right conduct was not some transcendent virtue but, precisely, what pharaoh and the Vizier decided. Even priests cultivated the virtues of silence or, as we should say, keeping a low profile.

A symptom of the society in which everything seems determined by authority or fate can be the belief in magic. Magic had always played an important part in Egyptian life. Now there was a greater reliance on spells, amulets, and supposedly miracle-working papyrus scrolls which could operate for good or ill depending on the 'witch' who made use of them. Even the state, which in earlier times had depended only on pharaoh's expressed will for the maintenance of order, now felt it necessary to threaten wrongdoers with supernatural punishment. To protect his desert settlement on the way to the gold fields Seti I had said of a prospective thief, 'Osiris shall pursue him, Isis shall pursue his wife, Horus shall pursue his children, and the great ones, the lords of the necropolis, shall make their reckoning with him.' A term of praise frequently applied to pharaohs and Viziers in the past was 'They knew everything that went on'. Now the gods themselves were invoked to smell out the man who had useful information but did not see fit to divulge it. The centralized, autocratic state, with its institutionalized temple religion, had unintentionally fostered private cults, an almost despairing emphasis on magic, and the need to crack down on wrongdoers and dissidents with threats of Lear-like extravagance: 'I will do such things – What they are yet I know not – but they shall be the Terrors of the earth!'

The temples were by now taking a disproportionate share of the national wealth so the priestly landowners grew richer, and possibly more indolent, as the peasants and even such employees of the state as necropolis workers became poorer. Temple granaries could be full while peasants and artisans starved. The official classes not only seemed blind to what was happening but were rapidly developing a philosophy that the state existed for priests and civil servants, not the other way round. Even soldiers who had created the new wealth of Egypt by plundering Asia were disparaged. All educated men underwent the training of a scribe and the texts set for copying in the school-room delighted in drawing attention to the miseries of the soldier's life. He is, they learned, beaten like a piece of papyrus, he goes on terrible campaigns, he falls ill and is brought home on the back of a donkey. The unremitting toil of the farmer was something no sensible man would put up with. There were dangers even in being a baker who might, it seems, fall into the oven. Choose to be a scribe, the propaganda went on, for in that way you will be spared a lot of disagreeable work with your hands. If generations of schoolboys were subjected to this kind of indoctrination it is no wonder Egypt was adminis-tered by men who did not think the good life had to be worked for but was a present from the gods. The danger to the state was ossification which, if the perfumed young men of Per-Ramesse ever talked about it, would seem incapable of arrest by mortal man. Hence cynicism, fatalism (a popular new story was about a prince who would die either by a crocodile, a snake or a dog and could in no way escape his destiny), magic games, and rather more drunkenness than at one time was thought socially acceptable.

It was a time for prose rather than poetry. The Tale of the Foredoomed Prince is one of a batch of stories that come from the Ramesside period in the new, more colloquially written Egyptian which Akhenaten more than anyone else was responsible for making respectable. Classical Egyptian of the Middle Kingdom was as different from the Egyptian spoken at Per-Ramesse as Latin is from Italian. The popular stories of the time are all written in this new Egyptian and if it is true that an understanding of a people is best arrived at through their popular entertainments, then these stories should be closely studied for they are the nearest we shall get to the diversions of the ancient Egyptians. They had a great sense of fun, and they loved the deflating anecdote.

The Tale of the Two Brothers is interesting from another point of view. It is a clear anticipation of the story of Joseph and Potiphar's wife in Genesis 39. Hand in hand with the literary realism that the new Egyptian made possible went an irreverence for the gods and the other powers that be. Talking about the gods as though they were fallible humans is a very ancient Egyptian characteristic but there is nothing from earlier times quite so deflating as the story saying how a tribunal of the gods adjudicated in the matter of whether Seth or Horus should be king of Egypt. At one point the king of the gods, Re, is so hurt by the insults thrown at him by the monkey-god Bab that, like Achilles, he retired to his tent and sulked. The gods then sent Hathor, the goddess of love, to soften him by her amorous advances. It is broad and bawdy farce, rather like Boccaccio. Even the military prowess of the warrior pharaoh is held up to gentle ridicule in a cartoon about the great battle between the cats and the mice.

Another popular piece of writing tells of the controversy between two officials, Hori, who had an important job in the royal stables, and Amenemope, who was a senior administrator in the army. Amenemope had, it appears, written a pert letter to Hori in reply to some criticism of the way he had carried out his responsibilities; he had even made great claims to knowledge and experience. Hori's lengthy reply is mockery. Let me test your knowledge and experience, he says. How many bricks are there in a ramp of such-and-such dimensions? How do you estimate the weight of an obelisk and how many men will, as a result of your calculations, be needed to drag it on a sled? You are, said Hori, supposed to be a military administrator but you don't even know how to work out the rations for a division of five thousand men. And as for Syria and Palestine, about which you claim to know so much, answer the following questions. Have you been in Lebanon where the sky is dark by day, the road overgrown with trees of all kinds, cypresses, oaks, and cedars? Tell me, what sort of place is Byblos? And so on, in a mixture of contempt and raillery.

He takes us on an itinerary that passes through many of the famous places from northern Syria down to the Egyptian border. He is anxious to explore Amenemope's pretensions to being a *mahir*, a Canaanite word which had come to mean an experienced traveller. He wanted to demonstrate that he, Hori, really was a *mahir*. Consequently he bludgeons Amenemope with information about the fierceness and size of Beduins who lie in ambush, the hazards of driving a chariot along a mountain track with a ravine on one side and the mountain on the other, the numbers of lions, panthers, and hyenas that have to be braved, and the beautiful girls of Joppa who have to be braved in a different way.

One imagines Hori setting all this down in a high state of excitement, breaking off now and again to shout with laughter and call over one of his friends to listen to the latest taunt he has been able to think of. As a counterbalance to the view that is formed from tombs and temples it should be remembered that the bruising high spirits of Hori are as characteristically Egyptian as the obsession with mortuary rites and grave furniture. They were preoccupied with death because they loved life so much and wanted it to go on for ever, sowing and harvesting, hunting, growing flowers, drinking beer, and anointing themselves. The Egyptians were the great jokers of the Bronze Age and in a way that reminds one of the boisterous geniality of some modern blacks from East Africa.

The eastern Mediterranean area, including Anatolia, the Aegean, and North Africa, seems to have entered an arid phase in the last quarter of the second millenium. This was as much the reason as anything else for the increasingly vigorous demands made by the Libyans to come in from the desert and settle in the Delta with its unfailing supply of water and food. There was famine in parts of the Hittite confederacy and grain was shipped from Egypt to meet the emergency. Migrant pastoralists in the hill countries south and east of the Dead Sea, Edom and Moab, failed to find the usual grazing which the previously regular winter rains had made possible and some of them, like the Israelites, moved into Egypt. A frontier official reported that he had allowed tribesmen of Edom to pass the frontier fortress and come to the pools of Pithom so that they and their flocks might live 'through the good pleasure of pharaoh'.

Such was the enthusiasm with which Ramesses pressed on with the building of his new city that his overseers recruited labour where they could. Contemporary letters describe how Per-Ramesse acted as a magnet for people. Peasants who could manage it left the land and found pleasanter niches as servants or storekeepers but even so there was a shortage of labour for construction work. Tribesmen who wandered in from Sinai were exposed to the danger of forced labour and this is what happened to the Israelites. Few scholars nowadays believe that all twelve tribes underwent the Egyptian bondage, probably only the tribe of Benjamin and certain families from the tribe of Levi, who became more Egyptianized than most, no doubt from longer residence.

However many tribesmen there were, and whether they were from only two tribes or more, there is no doubt that building mud-brick houses would have come very strange to them for they were tent-dwellers. Setting them to make bricks, with or without chopped straw (needed to bind the baked mud together), would have caused the special kind of resentment that comes from having to carry out meaningless tasks. No doubt, too, the Egyptian overseers could be merciless task masters, just as they were with Egyptian peasants called up for the traditional *corvée*. The Israelites naturally wanted to get out, particularly as in Moses (an Egyptian name, incidentally) they had found a leader who said a certain god called Yahweh would save them.

If an Egyptian military force set out in pursuit of the absconding labour force there is a good chance they would have run into trouble. The marshes were extensive and the lakes many. The Egyptians who had little topographical interest unless it was related to some practical consideration would, with their horses and chariots, be more likely to get bogged down than the tribe of Benjamin with their trotting donkeys. Even so it was a near thing. There was no dividing of the Red Sea but there almost certainly was an escape so miraculous that the tribesmen attributed it to divine intervention.

Ramesses is the most likely candidate for the pharaoh of the Exodus but he would not in person have taken any part in the pursuit of the Israelites. It is not entirely fanciful to imagine him voicing his displeasure at the news that a whole section of chariotry and their standard bearer had come to grief in the reedy marshes. If he had been present the Beduin would never have got away; he knew the area well from expeditions in his papyrus boat to catch fish and knock down duck with his boomerang. But let the Beduin go. Ramesses doubted whether they were right for building work anyway. They would be back when the next dry summer came.

As was traditional Ramesses celebrated his first jubilee or *Sed* festival in the thirtieth year of his reign when he was still not fifty, and then went on to celebrate another eleven or twelve of them at varying intervals. His son Khaemuast, High Priest of Ptah, organized many of these festivals for him and we can be sure they were on a lavish scale. Ramesses could quite reasonably regard his jubilee as a genuine cause for national rejoicing. He was the state. He was vigorous and confident. It therefore followed that Egypt was flourishing.

When he took off his cloak and stepped from under the canopy into the hot sunshine carrying a sceptre and whisk, wearing nothing but a short kilt with an animal's tail hanging behind, he could see all the gods of Egypt in booths before him. Pennants and streamers lifted in the breeze. White-robed priests began a hymn of praise and thanksgiving. As he started to run it would not have crossed his mind that he was doing anything the least bit undignified. He was reaffirming the unity of the Two Lands in the most unambiguous way possible by running round them. He could persuade himself he was running round the real Egypt and not just round a symbolic track. As he did not take a great deal of exercise these days he began to sweat. Here he was, spending himself again for the good of Egypt, as he had all alone spent himself at Kadesh, now running his ritual four courses while everyone else just stood and watched. As they had stood and watched at Kadesh. He had been by himself then too. Quite shining with sweat he now approached the booth of the wolf-god Upuaut and for some reason he could not immediately remember, though it had been explained to him by Khaemuast, offered his sceptre in the direction of the wolf emblem on its tall pole. It was something to do with the wolf province being instrumental in helping the first king to win the battle that led to national unity. Perhaps troops from the province came under their wolf standard at just the right moment, as the task force from Amurru had arrived at Kadesh. That, too, had ended well. The rest of his life would be one long *Sed* festival and Ramesses saw himself running and sweating for ever, quite alone.

He considered that good fortune was what he was entitled to. Luck seems never to have deserted him, even in such a small matter as the digging of a well. In Nubia his father Seti had dug a dry well but Ramesses, in his turn, ordered another well to be sunk in the same area. As he had confidently expected, the labourers struck water almost immediately.

8
LIBYAN WARS AND THE PEOPLES OF THE SEA

THE MAN WHO LET THE TRIBES IN FROM
Edom to the pools of Pithom was an officer in the Medjay force, which had
by now evolved from a mainly Nubian body of light-armed auxiliaries serving
with the army into one largely Egyptian responsible for internal security including the guarding of tombs and also working as a frontier patrol. Part of
their time might be spent on the Sinai frontier in the east, part on the Libyan
frontier, particularly the sector north from Memphis and along the coastal
strip as far as Mersah Matruh. Of the two postings the Sinai one was less
subject to local alarms, for the Semitic tribesmen who came in and out of
Egypt were peaceable. But service with the Medjay meant being sent to re-
mote.localities on the Rafia road where there were no diversions and boredom
could easily set in. 'I spend the whole day watching the birds,' wrote one poor
fellow posted out in Sinai. 'There is the gnat at sunset and the midge at noon.
The sandfly stings and sucks at every vein.' Longing for the delights of Joppa
or, more frequently, Egypt, the exile set reed to papyrus. 'I want to sleep all
the time. Please god, take me to Memphis!'

It was different in the west. Patrolling the western approaches to Egypt did
not prompt such longing, partly because it was from a base in the Delta and
the rangers did not feel so cut off but mainly because they had to deal with a
different kind of intruder, the Libyans, and there was no time for boredom.
The Libyans were armed with bows, javelins, and even chariots of a heavy,
lumbering kind. Unlike the Asiatic pastoralists they were not organized in
tribes but in larger communities headed by a senior chief capable of gathering
a considerable army. Going from east to west, from the Delta to Cyrenaica,
there were a number of these Libyan peoples: first of all the Tehenu, then the
Libu, and finally the Meshwesh. They fought each other from time to time
over wells and grazing rights but the main movement of all of them was east-
ward into the Delta where they could graze their cattle and grow their barley
with greater assurance of success than in their arid homelands. Another
Libyan people, the Temehu, were based on oases from Siwa in the north down
through Farafra, Dakhla, and the great oasis of Kharga to Nubia, where they
traded for ivory. Sometimes they raided across to Thebes itself. Libyans kept
the Egyptian frontier force on its toes.

Previous page : Libyan and Philistine prisoners-of-war in their characteristic
head-dresses being led in triumph to Amon-Re by Ramesses III

The Libyans were dark-skinned, rather lanky people with some, particularly in the north, who were fair-headed and blue-eyed, the result of migration across the Mediterranean. They were hunters and cattle-raisers, growing barley where they could and speaking a number of languages of which modern Berber is a survivor. Judging by the way they were represented in Egyptian art the men wore their hair braided with a prominent side-lock, they were bearded (in contrast to the Egyptians), and like tribesmen in hot countries the whole world over they went naked but for a cloak, perhaps of skin, and a decorative and prominently exhibited penis sheath. Their tents were also of skins or leather. Their population increased faster than the desert, the oases, and the cultivable margins of the Mediterranean could provide for and this pressure of population on resources was increased by moves from the west to Cyrenaica where the Meshwesh had been reinforced by immigration from the Aegean.

Invasion from Libya had been a common feature of Egyptian life for some time. Both Seti I and Ramesses II undertook campaigns against the intruders that led to captives being 'presented to Amon'. When Ramesses took the field against them he found the Tehenu strengthened by the Vikings of those days, the Sherden, who, after their defeat, were conscripted into the Egyptian army. Ramesses regularly did this, particularly for use in areas where the Libyans and Sherden could not make common cause with the local inhabitants. Four thousand of them were sent on an expedition through the Wadi Hammamat towards the Red Sea to deal with bandits threatening the gold supply. Even though Libyans were actually settled in some numbers in the Delta the pressure from the west became greater rather than less. The danger came to a head during the reign of Ramesses II's son, Merneptah.

Merneptah cannot originally have had regal expectations but his father lived so long that all his elder brothers died and he found himself pharaoh at the age of fifty or so. Quite early in his reign he had to deal with a Libyan invasion of more than usual danger. The leader, Meryey, had gathered together an army of up to twenty-five thousand fighting men and they advanced on the Delta with their families in ox-drawn carts and all their domestic kit, intent on occupying Egyptian land. The year was 1231 BC. Meryey was supported not just by North Africans but by contingents who, under their Egyptian names, can be identified as Achaean Greeks (the same people who within a few years were besieging Troy), the Etruscans before their migration to Italy, the Sherden, or Sardinians, and the Shecklesh who later went on to seize Sicily and gave their name to that island. There were Lycians, too, who had fought against Ramesses II at Kadesh.

The elderly Merneptah, as he moved his army towards the invading Libyans and their allies for the decisive battle, must have known that the Libyans were stiffened in a quite unusual way and the threat to Egypt was greater than at any time since the Hyksos. He did not take part in the battle

Hands and genitals cut from dead enemies are presented to Ramesses III

himself though Amon made an oracular patriotic pronouncement and Ptah appeared to pharaoh in a dream, handing him a scimitar with which to conquer. The tactics seem to have been to let the invaders consolidate their forces the better to deal with them in a major battle, rather than get caught up in skirmishes. The Egyptians delayed so long before making an assault that the Libyans, perhaps to their surprise, penetrated some way into the Delta where the battle of Perire was fought; nobody knows exactly where – one can only guess that they did not cross the Canopic branch of the Nile. The battle was won in six hours by superior fire-power. The Egyptian chariotry transported the archers with impunity to within three hundred yards of the Libyan line and then poured a fusillade into their ranks with their powerful composite bows. The Libyans could not get near enough for the hand-to-hand fighting in which they might have done well. After a while they began to break and fall back, only to be pursued by the chariotry, the chariotry runners and the infantry, 'Amon-Re being with them and Set giving them the land'.

Archers and spearmen of Ramesses III's army going into action

The Egyptians claimed six thousand dead and nine thousand prisoners. Meryey, who escaped with his life, lost his wives, his tents, his furniture, his oxen, goats, and donkeys. He was seen rushing past one of the Egyptian frontier forces from which it was subsequently reported that he had been deposed by his infuriated chieftains who believed the disaster was due to his poor generalship. Merneptah, plump and going bald, waited at Memphis for tidings of the battle and subsequently appeared on the palace balcony to inspect the fruit of victory. As was traditional, a piece of each dead Libyan – a hand from the circumcised and the phalli of those who did not observe this Egyptian and Semitic practice – was placed in baskets and paraded on donkeys. All this under a cloud of flies. It is something of a puzzle that dead Achaeans of Mycenaean Greece, the Akawasha, were treated as though circumcised, which does not accord with what we know from other sources. Meryey's supporters were drawn from a wide geographical area. Egyptian appreciation of the full extent of the international nature of the forces arrayed against them might not have arisen until after the battle had been fought and won, and mistakes could easily be made. The military scribe responsible for making the tally had probably confused the Akawasha with a Syrian contingent.

Egyptian relief at the victory was enormous. What they regarded as a terrible threat had been removed. People could now 'walk freely upon the road', said an inscription, and 'could sit down and chat with no fear in their hearts'. When messengers arrived they found the watchmen asleep but did not bother to wake them up. They themselves waited in the shade because the information they brought was of no urgency, as it would have been in time of war. The stela from which these words are taken then goes on to talk of Merneptah's other victories in Asia – Canaan plundered, Askelon 'carried off', Khatti pacified (obviously untrue), and indeed the whole of Syria and Palestine punished for rebellion. It also says, 'Israel is desolated, his seed is not.'

This stela found in Merneptah's funerary temple as recently as 1896 is known as the Israel Stela because of the reference to Israel, the only one to be found in Egyptian records, and pre-dating the writing of the Hebrew scriptures by several centuries. When it was discovered, it threw fundamentalist opinion into some confusion because Merneptah was believed by many to be the pharaoh of the Exodus, but here he is fighting Israel, already established as a people somewhere in Palestine. This is a state of affairs that could only have existed some considerable time after the Exodus. It was equally disconcerting to fundamentalist opinion when two years later, in 1898, Merneptah's mummy was discovered. According to Exodus he had been lost in the Red Sea and the only comfort was that the mummy showed traces of salt. Salt is found on all mummies because natron, which is used in the process of mummification, consists not only of soda and a number of other things but common salt as well. It was considered more pious to believe that the salt on Merneptah's mummy came from the Red Sea, from which the drowned pharaoh's body had been recovered.

Merneptah's reign was short, not more than ten years, and it was followed by a succession of even shorter reigns when there was rivalry and intrigue over the succession. This was the time when that other centre of power, the Temple of Amon at Karnak, consolidated its strength not only because of the resources at its command but because of the lack of any strong pharaoh who could take a grip on affairs. The priestly hierarchy at Thebes fell increasingly under the control of a group of high officials, usually related to each other, and for the first time this clan or family grouping gave promise of creating a state within the state. It required only the office of High Priest to become hereditary for the break-up of central authority in the state to come dangerously near realization, particularly if there was feuding among Ramesses II's descendants. That time was not just yet, though some think the ambitious High Priest Roma-Roy was the eldest son of the long-serving Bekenkhonsu. Final proof is lacking. Even comparatively modest jobs were passed on from father to son, so why not the High Priesthood? Inheritance was accepted, even expected, and it was certainly something Roma-Roy believed in.

He is an interesting figure in the politics of the time because he contended for power. The Egyptians are normally not credited with thinking analytically about power. There was no question of rendering unto Caesar what was Caesar's and unto God what was God's, for in the Egyptian state the monarch was a god; the profane and the sacred were indivisible not only in his person but in all human activities. Roma-Roy, however, was a sharp-minded man with little difficulty in understanding that Caesar did not necessarily have to be a god – after all the Hittites and Babylonians did not have divine kings – though he might well have conceded that such was the strength of Egyptian tradition that a nod in the direction of divine kingship was inevitable in the Nile valley. He would be perfectly happy to play the role of a conventional High Priest of Amon under a strong pharaoh; but if times changed and there was confusion at Memphis he would have other and more personal interests to serve. It seems characteristic of this man that he sometimes wrote his name as Roma and sometimes as Roy, so that a generation of Egyptologists thought he was not one man but two! So, in a sense, he was.

His time came after the death of Merneptah in 1214 BC. Merneptah's son, Seti III, ruled for six years. He had a remarkable wife, Tewosret, who outlived him. She also outlived his successor, a boy-king called Siptah, and a certain Amenmesses, who was in contention for the throne – successfully for a time. Supported by a Syrian called Bay, her 'Great Chancellor of the entire land' as he claimed, Tewosret outfaced whatever opposition there might have been and herself became Queen Regnant. It was a time when, to quote a document of some years later, 'the land of Egypt was cast adrift, every man a law unto himself. . . . Then another time came after it of empty years, when Arsu a Syrian was with them as prince and he made the entire land contributory under his sway.' Arsu may be none other than Bay, Queen Tewosret's Great Chancellor, under another name.

The events and personalities of the time are obscure. In one surviving papyrus there is even talk of civil war. One forms perhaps an exaggerated impression of the disarray into which the country fell after the death of Merneptah. The claims of a succeeding pharaoh could be misleading. But at least there must have been some slackening of central authority and Roma-Roy took advantage of this, like any ambitious prince-bishop of the Middle Ages. In the lifetime of Seti II he had presumed to have his image, his name, and his achievements inscribed on the walls of the Karnak temple. For a mere High Priest this was unprecedented. Before the Akhenaten schism the presumption would have been regarded as sacrilegious; only the name and achievements of pharaoh appeared on temple walls. In contrast to the warlike achievements of pharaoh, Roma-Roy had nothing more earth-shaking to record than his rebuilding of the temple bakery but he extracted as much kudos from it as Tuthmosis III did from taking a fortified city. Roma-Roy accompanied the record of his achievement with thanksgiving for his long life (he was High Priest for twenty-five years), for the fact that his sons and grandsons were all priests at Karnak, and with his expression of the hope that one of them might follow him in his own high office which, he asked of Amon, might be in hereditary succession for ever.

Roma-Roy had his son Bekenkhonsu as Second Prophet. (That he had the same name as the High Priest in Ramesses II's time is the main reason for thinking Roma-Roy was the old man's son.) He had a grandson as Fourth Prophet and his nephew was Third Prophet. So all the major priesthoods were in the hands of the same family. He was also related by marriage to a family that later produced mayors of Thebes. It so happened that when Roma-Roy died he was not succeeded by a son because the family backed the losing side in the succession dispute and Seti II appointed his own nominee, Mahuhy, his secretary. It was a little too early for High Priests to follow through to their logical conclusion the kind of claim that was expressed in the picture of Roma-Roy on the temple walls but he had created an expectation in the sacerdotal establishment that a family succession was possible. It was merely postponed.

This was because a strong man with the name of Sethnahkte took over and established a new dynasty, the Twentieth. He was quickly followed by his exceptionally able and energetic son who, as it turned out, was to be the last of the warrior pharaohs, the last whose name has anything of the resonance of his famous predecessors, Ramesses III. The new pharaoh had the greatest admiration for the achievements of his illustrious predecessor (and probably his ancestor too through a female line), Ramesses II, and he set out quite deliberately to imitate his example, by building magnificently and, not least, by trimming the pretensions of the priesthood of Amon. Roma-Roy had been called – or called himself – 'chief of the prophets of all the gods of Upper and Lower Egypt' but his successor under Ramesses III had to be content with leaving out the reference to Upper and Lower Egypt.

It is mildly surprising that Roma-Roy's name was suffered to remain on the walls of the Karnak temple. The priesthood of Amon could scarcely have objected to its removal. Being intelligent men they would have realized that the supreme question for Egypt now was not so much the status of their High Priest but whether the wheel of power and empire had come full circle and whether, four hundred years after Amosis had disposed of the Hyksos, the country was to be conquered by a new lot of foreigners.

After the fall of Troy the Greeks sailed home again, according to Homer, by the most extraordinarily circuitous routes. The wanderings of Odysseus are part of literature but the supposed voyages were based on real voyages; Homer made use of the sea-lore of his time and the landfalls are recognizable even today. Odysseus went to Libya, Phoenicia, and Egypt where he took part in a piratical raid. Homer tells how these buccaneers ran their ships on to the shore and climbed the dunes to reconnoitre the low-lying land behind. It was a characteristic Delta landscape they saw, with fields of barley, grazing cattle, and, whenever the ground was high enough to be above flood level, villages of mud-brick houses with whitewashed pigeon-cotes standing in groves of date palm. The raiders attacked one of these villages, killed a number of peasants, and were busy plundering when they were surprised by a detachment of soldiers with chariots sent out from the nearest fortress. Odysseus naturally got away but the rest were either speared or taken prisoner; they would end up as slaves or army conscripts. This is what happened to many a Sherden rover. Menelaus, too, went to Egypt and landed on the island of Pharos where he was led to believe that his return to Sparta had been delayed because of his failure to sacrifice to the gods. The real explanation is that his adventures and those of Odysseus are an interpretation of what lingered in the folk memory of the real piratical raids and salt-water migrations at the end of the second millenium BC. The Egyptians called the invaders 'The Peoples of the Sea'. Among them were four new names: the Tjekker and the Philistines of the Bible, the Denyen (who were probably Homer's Danaoi) and the Weshesh.

Ramesses III who successfully fought them off is a tantalizing figure. For all his great achievements there is an almost Hamlet-like uncertainty and melancholy about some of his behaviour, due to an awareness perhaps of the long-term problems that still faced the country. There are two main sources of information about the wars he fought with the Libyans and the Sea Peoples: the great and still impressive temple of Medinet Habu which he built in western Thebes and the Harris Papyrus in the British Museum which is nearly forty-five metres long and so called because soon after its discovery in 1855 on the floor of an ordinary rock tomb under a heap of mummies it was bought by a Mr A. C. Harris of Alexandria.

In spite of their defeat by Merneptah twenty years before, the Libyans, under the pressure of dire necessity and the ambitions of the most westerly tribes, particularly the Meshwesh, had continued to infiltrate into the Delta. Under a new leader, a certain Themer, they now moved to attack Egypt, taking as their pretext the supposed decision by Ramesses III to impose a new leader, a mere child, upon them. The Libyans already settled in the Delta and the various Sea Peoples who had landed strong contingents could be expected to contribute to the muster. Ramesses, who may have spent more of his time in the south at Thebes than his more immediate predecessors, was content to wait until the invaders, thirty thousand strong, began 'sitting in Egypt', to quote the inscription, and became careless with success. At Karnak, Amon handed Ramesses a scimitar with which to fight and the ensuing battle in the Delta was like Perire all over again with the difference that on this occasion pharaoh was present and charged in his chariot. He claimed to have killed vast numbers of the enemy in person and taken a thousand or so prisoner – red-bearded men with side-locks and rather elaborately worked cloaks. They were branded with pharaoh's name, like cattle, and enslaved.

This was in the fifth year of Ramesses' reign. Six years later they were back again, this time led by the Meshwesh, who were clearly a determined and racially self-conscious people for they survived the disaster that Ramesses inflicted on them and were mentioned by Herodotus some six hundred or more years later as the Maxyes, who by that time had moved west to the neighbourhood of Tunis. But now, in 1187 BC, their object was to settle in Egypt. The Meshwesh and their chief allies, the Libu, were not, incidentally, on good terms with the most easterly Libyans, the Tehenu, who encouraged them to go ahead with their attack on the Egyptians in the hope they would be taught a lesson, as indeed they were.

For a time the Egyptians were on the defensive and had to fight a delaying action based on two fortresses, one of them called Hatsho which was on a canal known as the Waters of Re which ran north from the Fayoum as a continuation of the Bahr el Yusif. It was well within the Delta, surrounded by farm land and a dozen miles or so from the desert's edge. Once again the superior fire-power and discipline of the Egyptians was too much for the Libyans and when the main battle took place they were quite simply crushed. The chief of the Meshwesh was taken prisoner and killed in spite of an appeal from his father.

This was the last armed immigration by the Libyans. Ramesses proclaimed an annual festival to be called 'Slaying the Meshwesh', prisoners were conscripted into the armed forces, their women and children in 'tens of thousands' drafted into slavery, and their cattle 'in number like hundreds of thousand' went to augment the herds of Amon, in gratitude for the victory-winning scimitar. The figures may well be exaggerated but they do underline the fact that these incursions from the western desert were folk-movements typical of other migrations that were taking place in Asia and Europe at that time.

Unlike the Libyans the Sea Peoples were successful to the extent that one major contingent, the Peleset or Philistines, gave their name to the part of the Levant they succeeded in permanently occupying, Palestine. They came by land and sea. By land they travelled from Anatolia into Syria with their families and household goods in waggons drawn by oxen; their eventual objective was Egypt, that fabled land where grain was abundant and the donkeys kicked up gold nuggets as they trotted. By sea they came from Crete, a land the Israelites were so convinced was their homeland that they called the *negeb* where they settled 'the Cretan South'. They were skilled smelters of ore and metal workers, particularly of iron, with secrets they did not want others to share – with the Israelites, for example. In Samuel 1:13 it is stated that no smith (of iron) was found throughout all the land of Israel, 'lest the Hebrews make them swords or spears'. It was the beginning of the age of iron. The metal was not unknown in Egypt – there were iron daggers in Tutankhamon's tomb, probably of Hittite origin – but whereas bronze could be beaten cold, the shaping of iron involved beating the metal red-hot, a more complicated process requiring new skills which the Egyptians were slow to learn. With iron, great two-edged swords could be made and used for slashing and thrusting in a way no existing Egyptian bronze weapon could.

The naval victory of Ramesses III over the Sea Peoples, here Philistines with their feathered or possibly leather head-dresses

Ramesses was convinced that the great pincer movement on Egypt was a conspiracy. He declared that foreigners in their islands to the north – he was still unclear that Anatolia was not a group of islands – had plotted to invade Egypt. No land could stand against them. Khatti, Cyprus, Arzawa, and the city states of Syria, Carchemish, and Qode had already fallen. But the Egyptian army and navy was rapidly being prepared for the onslaught. In the end he had to fight two battles, the first a land battle somewhere in Syria and another, some time later, the crucial engagement which has been described as the first naval engagement in history. It is certainly the first to be fully recorded. Judging by the evidence provided on the walls of Medinet Habu it took place in the Pelusiac branch of the Nile, some distance north of Per-Ramesse, where it entered the Mediterranean.

On land the Sea Peoples fought in the Hittite manner, from chariots with two armed men and a driver. Their sea-going boats had no oarsmen, were powered by sail alone, and had prows that ended in carved ducks' heads whose bills served as battering rams. A sea-borne invasion of Egypt with ships that could be moved only under sail would be a hazardous undertaking even when the Egyptians were taken by surprise, as on this occasion they were not. The

Egyptian fleet shadowed the ships of the Sea Peoples into 'the river mouths' of the Delta. The long, crescent-shaped Egyptian craft were powered by sail and up to twenty-four oarsmen. Having superior manoeuvrability they were able to get to windward and trap the invading fleet against the shore, where strong contingents of bowmen were waiting for them. The Philistines in their head-dresses of leather and horsehair, with their Tjekker or Danaoi allies, were trapped between the Egyptian marines on their ships, armed with bows and javelins, and the bowmen on the shore. After they had taken a heavy toll the Egyptian ships were able to move in, ram the helpless invading ships, seize them with grappling hooks, and engage the enemy in hand-to-hand fighting. 'A net,' Ramesses said, 'had been prepared for the enemy.' They fell into it, and were butchered without mercy.

Above : A faience plaque of different types of prisoners taken by Ramesses III. Opposite : This unique gateway to Ramesses III's palace and temple complex of Medinet Habu is inspired by the migdol fortresses encountered by the Egyptians in Palestine and Syria

His victory no doubt was a great one, but to claim, as he did, that he then settled the defeated Sea Peoples in Palestine, in the land of Canaan, is probably a self-regarding way of saying he had little alternative. He could scarcely have been easy in his mind about making the cities of Gaza, Askalon, Ashdod, and Dor their responsibility, as he did; the Philistines and Tjekker answered to pharaoh, that is to say, for the defence of these cities and for the raising of tribute. The effect was to give the Sea Peoples time to put down roots in their new homeland, where they came to flourish as merchants, traders, and warriors and to provide, in time, the means of shutting the Egyptians out of Asia. At home, however, Ramesses had established such order and such a sense of security that he claimed women could walk wherever they pleased with no danger of molestation, soldiers and the chariotry lost their occupation and foreign conscripts, the Sherden and the Kehek, were able to relax at night, stretching full length in their beds with no fear of attack. No one could have been more aware than Ramesses III himself that for a variety of reasons Egypt was withdrawing into itself. These reasons included the economic and political inertia induced by the increasingly powerful priesthood of Amon, a disinclination to think internationally and really control the vigorous new vassals who had established themselves in Palestine, and an afternoon lethargy after a morning of effort.

His great monument, Medinet Habu, is the best preserved of all funerary temples but there is something self-conscious about it, rather as though Ramesses was saying that this is what a great pharaoh should do. How would it look in the final calendar of the gods? Compared with the precise inscriptions of Tuthmosis III, the language in which Ramesses III set out his achievements three hundred years later is rhetoric inflated to the point of meaninglessness. We cannot be sure that some of the campaigns credited to him actually took place; many were recorded in imitation of what Ramesses II had done. It has one feature unique in Egypt, a stone gatehouse built in imitation of a Syrian fortress, a *migdol*, of a kind the Egyptians had met ever since Amosis embarked on his first campaigns in Djahi. The purpose of this mimic fortress at Medinet Habu was not defensive or, indeed, military in any way. Some of the internal decorations in a large chamber upstairs have given the impression that pharaoh used it to receive specially favoured ladies of the harem. If Ramesses had intended to build something that would pay tribute to the Syrian campaigns of his ancestors and predecessors, and indeed of himself, and to the many Egyptian and Nubian dead whose bones lay under Asian sand and rock, this *migdol* in western Thebes could scarcely have been bettered.

Two views of Ramesses III's funerary complex at Medinet Habu, which epitomizes the strength of the empire in its latter days. The gatehouse modelled on a Syrian migdol *can be seen in the centre of the lower picture*

It is a memorial of Egypt's imperial effort. Hindsight gives an elegiac colouring to Ramesses III. Romantic historians begin to talk about the glory of Egypt departing, which is not entirely true, because later pharaohs achieved much; but after Ramesses III, the empire as Tuthmosis III had dreamed of it was gone and Egypt was on the defensive. If there is one building that stands for the four hundred years of Egyptian aggressiveness in the middle and late Bronze Age it is this fortified gatehouse of Medinet Habu where such ancient warriors as Ahmose, son of Ebana, Ahmose-Pennekheb, and that council of officers who sat with Tuthmosis III before Megiddo might meet in ghostly conclave to boast of what once had been.

Of all the imperial pharaohs it is surprising that Ramesses III should be the one whose life was threatened by a palace conspiracy. He was and it was very serious. It started in the harem and had as its object the murder of Ramesses III and the setting on the throne of one of his sons who was not the obvious successor. But who was the Crown Prince? One of the peculiarities of Medinet Habu is that the king's sons are shown there but they have no names against them, rather as though Ramesses had decided that only history would determine who was in the legitimate line of succession and who was not. It is not the least of the indications that he was psychologically odd. The conspiracy was provoked by uncertainty about the succession and at the centre of it was one of the king's wives, Tiy, who was ambitious that her son should be placed on the throne. At the trial his name was given as Pentaware, but it was not his real name.

The king had more than one harem. The one where the conspiracy was hatched accompanied the king on his travels and its chief administrator was a man called Paibekkamon. He was the chief link between Tiy, other women in her immediate circle, and their relatives outside, urging them in the most incredibly incautious way to stir up trouble against pharaoh. Even a troop-commander stationed in Nubia, brother of one of the harem women, was appealed to. In spite of the circumstantial account of the conspiracy in the papyrus records there is a curious air of unreality about it all. How could the twenty-nine conspirators, including scribes and other harem officials, have hoped to get away with it? A plot that involved, as this one did, people as lowly as the wives of door-keepers could not have been kept secret, particularly when black magic, involving spells and images in wax, was used to bring about pharaoh's downfall. This meant specialists had to be brought in. Yet one cannot doubt that the plot took place as described and was not some piece of cautionary fiction.

The conspirators made up a cosmopolitan community characteristic of the times; some of the most eminent people in the country were by now of foreign

The treasure chambers of the hypostyle hall at Medinet Habu still have part of their original roof intact

origin. One of the harem Butlers (a very senior post) was a Lycian, another was a Libyan; of the twelve judges at the trial at least two were not Egyptians, but they were all court officials and that is another point of interest. Why was a charge of high treason not judged by the highest authorities in the land? The Vizier was not involved in any way, certainly not Ramesses himself. Earlier in the reign of Ramesses III the Chief of the Workmen at Deir el-Medina was murdered in a dispute over who should eventually succeed him (he had no son to inherit the job as was customary) and the investigation was carried out by the Vizier Hori himself, no less. Odd that the murder of a workman, even a Chief Workman, should be the concern of the Vizier while the attempted assassination of a king was tried by palace officials. Perhaps it was wished to play down the importance of the affair by emphasizing its domestic nature but in that case why was it not hushed up but made the subject of a full official report placed in the temple-library at Medinet Habu? Even if that report was not authorized by Ramesses III himself but by his son, Ramesses IV, the question remains.

Five of the twelve judges got into trouble by having a merry party with some of the accused women. A lot of beer was drunk. This does not give the impression the judges were taking the plot all that seriously or that they were much in awe of pharaoh. Higher authority decided their behaviour was intolerable. One was told to kill himself, three had their noses and ears cut off, and the fifth, a standard bearer in the army, was let off with a severe reprimand. Some of the conspirators had false and offensive names ascribed to them in the report of the proceedings, presumably as a mark of contempt – Mesedsure, for example, which means 'Re hates him', and Binemuast, 'Wicked in Thebes'. The prince who was set up to succeed Ramesses if the conspiracy had succeeded was not given one of these pejorative names but Pentaware is a pseudonym. He and his mother, Tiy, suffered, in the words of the papyrus, 'their punishment to overtake them'. In other words they were probably allowed to commit suicide, together with five others in the conspiracy. Seventeen were condemned to death and executed by having their backs and necks broken with heavy blows.

Ramesses III, once he had set up the trial, washed his hands of the whole affair, requiring only that justice was done, not even wanting to be told what the outcome might be. The explanation usually given for this extraordinary detachment is that the account was written after his death – 'being in the presence of Osiris, the Ruler of Eternity' – on the authority of his son and successor, Ramesses IV, who did not wish his father to run the risk of divine retribution for any injustice unwittingly committed at the trial. So he invented and wrote in this self-exculpating behaviour. The account was certainly written after Ramesses' death which some have taken to mean that the conspiracy was successful; but if the king had been murdered the conduct of the trial would scarcely have been so relaxed that five of the judges would get caught up in a drinking party. A more plausible view is that Ramesses survived the plot but was so grieved and shocked by domestic treachery from a woman he had presumably once loved and from a youth who was, after all, his own son that he wanted to shut it and their necessary punishment out of his consciousness. Hence the inefficient way the trial was rapidly set up and the evident lack of seriousness with which nearly half the judges took their responsibilities. Ramesses was such a tolerant and moody man they just could not believe the capital charges would be pressed home. Whatever the truth of the matter the Harem Conspiracy of Ramesses III does seem to indicate a more general malaise to which the king's own disposition may have contributed and which can also be detected in the administrative shortcomings evident particularly towards the end of his reign.

The government simply failed in its obligation to provide the Deir el-Medina workmen with the grain and other rations which were their wages. In 1170 BC these necropolis workers declared they were starving and actually went on strike, the most ancient industrial dispute on record. It went on for months. Eventually, still not having received their dues, the workmen staged a sit-in at the Ramesseum. The Chief of Police made promises to them which he then failed to honour, so they launched an appeal to the Vizier who made a soothing and inadequate response. Eventually the mayor of Thebes, presumably in desperation, provided fifty sacks of grain from the offerings made to the Ramesseum. The temple, it will be noted, had resources others lacked. Interestingly enough the workmen regarded this diversion of temple offerings as sacrilegious, even though it was to benefit them, and lodged a complaint with the High Priest of Amon. The cry had even been raised that there was serious malpractice and that crimes were being committed in 'this place of pharaoh'. Malpractice seems the only feasible explanation. Granary overseers were corruptly trading the grain for their own benefit. Everyone from the Vizier downwards knew what was going on but no one, not the Vizier himself, not the High Priest of Amon, not the Great Butler nor the Chief Treasurer of pharaoh seemed capable of ensuring that the starving workers received their barley and wheat, except late and not in proper measure. The trouble went on for years.

The economy was based on a complicated barter system rather than anything that could be properly described as money. Nevertheless the value of goods, from slaves to barley, was related to certain weights of copper, gold, and silver. For most of Ramesses III's reign the value of a sack of emmer wheat was a deben (about ninety-one grammes) of copper but by the time of the workmen's strike it had moved up a little, to say one hundred grammes of copper. Real inflation did not take hold for another ten years but then the price of grain really shot up and the cost in human misery can only be guessed at. So long as Egypt had an empire and could exact, either in tribute or more normally through trade, the key imports of timber, silver, tin, and now the new metal iron, by exporting gold, linen, papyrus, and grain all was well. But now the ancient barter system that had served Egypt so well began to collapse. The country was importing materials such as iron for which she had to pay increasingly in gold and grain, and gold was not so plentiful as once it had been. Some increase in population may have put pressure on the supply of grain. Iron was gradually replacing bronze as the armament of the times. Inflation and economic disruption, that is to say, were brought about by maladministration, by a shift of emphasis from copper and the other natural products of Egypt to iron, and by the way wealth was tied up in the temples. Egypt has a good supply of iron ore and if the Egyptians had been possessed of intellectual curiosity and drive they would have exploited the fact and moved over from a copper-based civilization to an iron-based one with less anguish than in fact they did. They did not bother to find out what wealth there was for the taking – largely because the dominant ideology of the time was the priestly service of the gods and this was exploitative rather than wealth-creating. The Egyptian ascendancy internationally coincided with the time when copper in its amalgam with tin as bronze was the basic utilitarian metal. The Egyptian empire faded as iron came in.

The great Harris Papyrus is important not only for the information it gives about Ramesses III's Libyan wars and the shutting out of the Peoples of the Sea. It provides a detailed record of the wealth of the Egyptian temples at this time when the empire of Amon-Re was petering out. One way of looking at the record is as a bill presented by the god for services rendered. Ramesses died at about sixty-five years of age after he had been ruling for some thirty-one years, in (it has been conjectured) 1151 BC. In that year the document was drawn up at the direction of his son and successor Ramesses IV. It purports to list all the gifts made to the gods of Egypt – not just Amon-Re – during the dead king's long reign, and goes into the most extraordinary detail – everything from such comparatively unimportant items as fibre cords and sticks of cinnamon to vast quantities of barley, oil, herds of cattle, copper, silver, and gold. One item that catches the eye is Userhet, the gold-plastered sacred barque of Amon-Re. Quite a lot of this wealth was already in the hands of the temples at the time of Ramesses III's accession and he merely confirmed them in their possession of it; one example is the vineyard of Kankeme, renowned for its sweet red wine, which the god Amon had possessed in the Delta from the time of Ramesses II.

The statistics provided in the papyrus can be interpreted in different ways and have been much argued about. It does seem, however, that Ramesses III was by no means disproportionately generous to Thebes. But taking into account the established and inherited wealth of the temples, there is no doubt that Amon-Re had far and away the greatest share – something like 86 per cent of all the dues measured in units of silver. Amon-Re owned something like a quarter of all the cultivable land in Egypt – in addition to 9 towns in Syria,

56 in Egypt, 433 gardens, vineyards, and orchards (extra to ordinary cultivable land), 83 ships, nearly half a million cattle of all kinds, and over 86,000 artisans. The holdings of all the temples when aggregated amount to a third of the cultivable land and one-fifth of all the inhabitants. This must represent a substantial slice of the national wealth, and an even greater one if the tradition recorded in Genesis 47:26 is correct, and this wealth went untaxed. No one can be sure about this. Herodotus and Diodorus say it was not taxed, modern scholars say the exemption was limited and all the priests really got away with was the obligation to undertake forced labour, which existed from the time of the gods, mainly for the maintenance of the irrigation channels, the transport of blocks of masonry, and other such forms of *corvée*. It is clear, however, that the wealth of the temples was at the expense of the rest of the economy and that the mischief was compounded by inefficiency and corruption. In no other way is it possible to explain why the workmen of Deir el-Medina starved when the granaries of Amon were full. This was the main reason why the High Priest came to pay the royal workmen and so assumed the extra authority this implied. He supervised quarrying and distributed clothes, oil, fish (pay, that is) to people who should have been receiving it from pharaoh's agents. Economic strength brought power.

The question is why this prescription for misfortune was not more clearly seen by the state – by pharaoh and his Viziers, that is to say. Perhaps it is naïve to assume that the identification of a nation's problems lead to their solution when there are strongly entrenched vested interests who feel they have something to lose. This self-imposed impotence is what has caused national decline throughout the ages. But Ramesses IV seemed to have no understanding at all of the serious internal haemorrhage the country was suffering from. The whole thrust of the Harris Papyrus is the guarantee by the new pharaoh that he would honour all his father's munificence and do nothing to bring the wealth of the religious foundations into more general circulation.

He reigned for a mere six years and was followed by a succession of kings, all called Ramesses, one of whom at least was his brother, and none of whom reigned long, except for Ramesses XI. The picture is of a decline in royal power. Pharaoh spent most of his time in the Delta, far away from Thebes. At the same time there was a consolidation of the power and independence of the High Priest of Amon. Under Ramesses III the Chief Taxing-Master of the King and Steward of the Medinet Habu Temple lived to see his son, Ramesses-Nakht, become High Priest of Amon under Ramesses IV; he lasted into Ramesses VI's time and perhaps even Ramesses VII. Of his two sons one followed him in the High Priesthood – and this is the first time we can be really sure of the office being inherited – and the other came into his grandfather's job, Chief Taxing-Master of the King and Manager of the Lands of Pharaoh. Two non-royal brothers, that is to say, had in their hands the resources of Egypt and it is not surprising that one of them, Amenhotep the High Priest, should go beyond the presumption even of Roma-Roy and have his figure shown with pharaoh on the temple wall and on the same scale. The convention had always been to show pharaoh many times larger than anyone else (the queens of Amenophis III and Akhenaten were exceptions) but here the High Priest is not only as big as pharaoh, he actually upstages him by gesticulating and having a couple of thigh-high attendants to emphasize his own colossal stature. Ramesses IX, for it was in his reign this happened, is just a dummy. In the iconography of the time this signalled great alteration in the state.

9
AN EGYPTIAN ODYSSEUS

ONE OF THE GIFTS RAMESSES III MADE
to Amon-Re was a new boat, *Userhet*, a sacred barque, on which the god in his
shrine could go sailing on the Nile for his annual visits to the Harem of the
South and across to the west bank for his tour of the funerary temples. It was
a particularly splendid cedarwood barque over sixty metres long. The hull
was sheathed with gold to the water-line. The cabin-shrine amidships, too,
was overlaid with fine gold. The golden heads of rams were placed along the
side of the shrine, each wearing the uraeus-serpent emblem of royalty and the
high-feathered Atef crown. The intention was to make the barque rival the
sun itself in brilliance and at certain angles of the light it must indeed have
burned on the water with such intensity as to be painful to look at. Cedarwood is durable and provided it was regularly treated with one of the various
vegetable oils available there is no reason why it should not last many years.
But in course of time some of the timbers rotted and had to be replaced.
Perhaps they were so far gone an entirely new *Userhet* would have to be built.
There was only one place where the cedarwood could be obtained and that
was Lebanon.

Tuthmosis III would have demanded the cedarwood as tribute. Ramesses II
would have sent a royal envoy with a number of ships to Byblos, there to
negotiate a purchase – for times had changed and foreign goods were now
acquired by trade. But Ramesses had been dead for fifty years and there was
now no longer any central authority in Egypt. The country had passed
through a period marked by hardship for the poorest and danger for the
powerful. It was a time of galloping inflation in grain prices; measured by the
weight of copper needed to purchase a sack of grain the price of barley went
up 800 per cent in thirty years and emmer wheat 530 per cent. There were
struggles between different factions that led to actual fighting in the south of
the country, particularly round Thebes. What seems to have happened is that
Pinehas, the Viceroy of Nubia, stormed the fortified temple of Medinet Habu
and turned out the High Priest of Amon, only to be chased back to Nubia
by an army commander, Herihor, who became High Priest in turn.

As far south as Thebes there were raids from the desert by the ever-
persistent Libyans and Meshwesh, so that workmen in the necropolis area

*Previous page : The Lebanon provided Egypt with cedar and other woods
from the very earliest times*

dared not venture out to work. Such was the breakdown in any sense of national purpose that officials fraudulently misappropriated goods entrusted to them on a scale previously unheard of; tombs of kings and queens, tombs of nobles, of priests and viziers, were systematically robbed with the connivance of people in high places.

And now, when this need to replace the sacred barque arose at Thebes, there was no pharaoh on the spot to take an initiative; the last of the Ramesside pharaohs lived in political impotence at Memphis. The real power in the north was exercised by a one-time Vizier and army commander called Nesbenebded and his wife Tentamun, who were based at the new city of Tanis in the north-east of the Delta, while in Upper Egypt the soldier turned High Priest, Herihor, had such power he ruled as king in everything but name. Relations between Herihor and Nesbenebded were reasonably cordial but this may have been no more than a recognition of their mutual inability to interfere in the other's affairs. The centralized system set up in the wake of the Hyksos, with the god-king ruling over a society in which priests, army commanders, viziers, and other officials played allotted roles in life had fallen apart. How, then, did Egypt acquire cedarwood for holy work in Thebes?

The prince of Byblos at this time was Zakar-Baal, a shrewd and tough negotiator – as, indeed, he had to be to run a small state in the unsettled circumstances of the time. He had Egyptian functionaries, a Butler, for example, and Egyptian singing women in his entourage. He was a man capable of boasting that he had only to clap his hands and the cedar logs of Lebanon would lie on the shore at his feet. He lived in uneasy relationship with his neighbours and he was vulnerable to piratical raids by that branch of the Sea Peoples known as the Tjekker, who had established themselves down the Palestine coast at Dor. Nevertheless, in spite of all the uncertainties and new political alignments in Asia, Byblos had trading relations with Egypt that went back to the remotest times. Here, if anywhere in Asia, would be understanding of the propriety with which the god Amon-Re could make requests for support. Accordingly, and with some confidence, the 'elder of the portal of the Estate of Amon', the priest Wenamon, was despatched unaccompanied and with no great sum to pay for his expenses to see what he could do with Zakar-Baal.

Wenamon was a courageous and resourceful man who had no illusions about the unusual nature of his mission. Until fairly recently only pharaoh himself could authorize foreign missions; this one, to secure timber for the divine barque of Amon-Re, would be one in which pharaoh would take a special interest. But Ramesses XI counted for little nowadays and the real sponsor of the journey was the High Priest of Amon, Herihor. Wenamon would not have put it like that. He was the emissary not of a man but the god Amon-Re himself and to prove it he had an image of the god, known as 'Amon-of-the-Road', in a portable shrine which he kept covered by a curtain. Every day of his journey the shrine, in complete privacy, was opened, and the image treated with water, incense, and cosmetics in the same way as Herihor back in Karnak served the cult image in the temple every sunrise.

Wenamon could not have left Egypt without the approval and support of the real power in Lower Egypt, Nesbenebded of Tanis who controlled land routes and sea routes into the mouths of the Nile, and more particularly the still flourishing trade with the Phoenician seaboard, particularly Byblos, Tyre, and Sidon. Wenamon presented his credentials to Nesbenebded. The best that can be said is that he did nothing to impede Wenamon's departure but he did very little to help it either; the princely gesture would have been to provide a ship and escort. But reflecting, perhaps, that Amon-Re was not the divinity he once had been, Nesbenebded allowed Wenamon to depart, more or less as a private, fare-paying passenger on a ship – not an Egyptian one – that happened to be sailing for Phoenicia. What is more he retained Wenamon's credentials, knowing that without them Zakar-Baal would scarcely listen to Wenamon's importunings and would ask for authorization which only Nesbenebded could now supply. It was a little demonstration of power.

Wenamon's ship put into the Tjekker port of Dor, just south of the Carmel headland, not so very far from Yehem where Tuthmosis III had held his council of war before taking the Aruna road to Megiddo. Here, in contrast to that demonstration of Egyptian power, was a single priest going on what could not unfairly be described as a begging mission. In the harbour of Dor a member of the crew ran off with all his money. Wenamon's demand of the prince of Dor, Beder, that he should make this loss good was rejected on the grounds that the thief was a foreigner, from a foreign ship, and he, Beder, was not responsible in the way he would have been if the thief were a man of Dor. He did, however, provide him with food and drink, and Wenamon continued his journey. He was still so angry with Beder for failing to restore his lost money that when he eventually arrived at Byblos and found a Tjekker ship in the harbour, he went on board and, apparently by force, confiscated thirty *deben* of silver which he said he would keep until the thief at Dor was discovered and his property returned. As it is Wenamon who is telling the story we cannot be sure how much he is embroidering what actually happened.

There is no reason to doubt, however, that when he went ashore and pitched a tent to house himself and Amon-of-the-Road, Zakar-Baal was furious, thinking that he himself would now be subject to Tjekker reprisals. He ordered Wenamon to get out of his harbour. Wenamon said he could not go without a ship but it was clear that he was ready to use any stratagem to avoid being expelled. Zakar-Baal hesitated to use force and there was stalemate for twenty-nine days. After this time a youth in the town had an epileptic fit – it was supposed some god had put him in a frenzy – in the course of which he said to Zakar-Baal, 'Bring up the god Amon from the shore and the priest who is with him.' It is not impossible that Wenamon, the Egyptian Odysseus, had bribed the youth, for while the prophetic frenzy was at its height Wenamon was preparing under cover of darkness to embark, with Amon-of-the-Road, on a ship bound for Egypt, which is a strange coincidence. The harbour-master rushed down to stop him. The following morning Wenamon was ushered into the presence of Zakar-Baal who was seated in an upper chamber with his back to a window that gave on to the sea. So close was the palace to the sea, said Wenamon, that the waves of the great Syrian sea seemed to beat against the back of Zakar-Baal's head.

There now followed a conversation that reveals more about the decline of Egyptian power, and particularly of Amon's sway in Asia, than tombs and broken stelæ. Zakaar-Baal came to the point immediately. 'You claim to be on a mission from Amon. How am I to know that? Where are your credentials?' On being told that Wenamon had handed them over to Nesbenebded, the prince of Byblos threw his hands in the air. 'How do I know this is not some fraud? You sail into my harbour brought by a barbarian captain on a ship that is neither Egyptian nor of Byblos. There are twenty ships in the official syndicate trading with Egypt here and fifty more at Sidon. Why didn't Nesbenebded put you on one of those? It looks to me as though he simply wanted to get rid of you by having this ship's captain kill you and throw your body into the sea. But what am I to think? An emissary of Amon-Re does not travel as you have travelled.'

I kept silence at that great moment, Wenamon reported. It was a poignant silence. Even Zakar-Baal as he looked into the visiting priest's face must have thought of the dead past; and Wenamon, gazing at the waves, might have speculated what could have been done with a body of Nubian bowmen. There was little he could say to the angry Phoenician but he did his best. He explained his mission. He asked Zakar-Baal to give him cedarwood for the barque of Amon as his father had given it, and his father before him, as a tribute to the god. To which Zakar-Baal replied that he was no servant of Egypt and any timber supplied by him would have to be paid for. He spoke disparagingly of Egypt in the very place where at one time Rib-Addi had written to pharaoh, 'I prostrate myself seven times before my lord, my sun.' In his plea for armed support against those who were harassing him, Rib-Addi had written: 'Formerly, at the sight of a man from Egypt the kings of Syria and Canaan would flee before him' – a time, he might have added, when Egyptian troops had caroused in the fortified cities of their enemies, anointed themselves with sweet-smelling unguents, and made an Egyptian festival every day that they were there. Amon-Re, in his own chariot, had advanced at the head of the army to the Euphrates but now he was lodged in a tent on the seashore like some poor Beduin.

Zakar-Baal said that even if Wenamon was who he claimed to be, the journey he had come on was a silly waste of time. Amon-Re, as a god, was

The port of Byblos had such close links with Egypt over many centuries that the Egyptians called all sea-going boats, Byblos boats, regardless of their destination

played out. He had been a great god once, he had originated crafts and learning which had then spread to other lands. (Actually it is incredible that Zakar-Baal said this. More likely they are words put piously into his mouth by Wenamon for the benefit of Herihor back home.) But all that was a long time ago. Byblos had paid its debt. Any further tribute to the god would have to be on a strictly commercial basis.

Wenamon seems to have been stirred to a great declaration that he was on no foolish journey for although he had to spend twenty-nine days on the seashore Amon-Re was still king of the gods. He was still the universal god to whom all things were owed, the ships on the sea, Lebanon itself, even Zakar-Baal. What was this talk of payment by the Lord of All? Zakar-Baal's forefathers passed their lives making offerings to Amon. However, if Zakar-Baal insisted on being mercenary, let one of his officials go to Tanis with a message that Wenamon would write; he was quite sure that Nesbanebded would send whatever was required to pay for the cedarwood. He may have wondered privately whether this confidence was justified.

Zakar-Baal's pride must have been hurt by Wenamon's declaration that compared with his forefathers he was lacking in reverence for the supreme god; he agreed to send his scribe to Egypt and, by way of demonstrating his good intentions, said he was prepared to send also an advance consignment of timber, four hewn planks and wood for the keel, the prow, and the stern of the sacred barque. This he in fact did and Nesbanebded justified Wenamon's confidence by sending back four gold jars, a silver vessel, papyrus, linen, veils, mats, ox-hides, ropes, lentils, and baskets of fish, on the understanding he would be recompensed by Herihor at Thebes. Apparently this was enough to satisfy Zakar-Baal. Workmen were sent up into the hills to fell logs. After lying through the winter to season, they were dragged to the harbour and Zakar-Baal summoned Wenamon to inspect them with him. As they talked the shadow of Zakar-Baal's lotus fan fell on Wenamon and a court official with an Egyptian name, Penamon, said obscurely, 'The shadow of pharaoh your lord has fallen on you,' meaning possibly that Wenamon for all his apparent success was, like Egypt itself, facing a darkened future. Zakar-Baal told his official rather sharply to leave Wenamon in peace. He had made a characteristically tactless remark, of a sort you might expect from an expatriate Egyptian. Byblos itself faced too many uncertainties to joke about the future, Zakar-Baal could well have reflected.

For his part, Wenamon urged Zakar-Baal to set up a stela recording that at the behest of Amon-of-the-Road he had felled timber and sent it to Egypt in the hope that Amon would grant him fifty years of life beyond his normal span. The Phoenician did not appear to base any great expectation that his merits would be recognized in this way, for he replied in effect, 'That sounds impressive but they are only words.' He had, on the whole, behaved rather well to the emissary he had received with such scepticism; he may even have come to respect him. When the Tjekker arrived to arrest Wenamon because of his seizures of their thirty *deben* of silver, Zakar-Baal refused to let them act within his territories and Wenamon got away to Cyprus. But it had been a long, humiliating experience for a high Egyptian emissary and it is not surprising that, on his own confession, at one point he sat down and wept.

The account is so racy it has been taken for fiction. But there is no doubt that it is an actual account written by an official of the Temple of Amon-Re for the benefit of Herihor, the High Priest and effective ruler of Upper Egypt, in about 1100 BC. It should be read in the original text, of which the account given here is an interpretation. The detail fits other information available on the eastern Mediterranean at this time; and the portrait of Zakar-Baal and the experiences Wenamon went through have an air of painful authenticity. It is the most dramatic rendering we have of the repute in which Egypt was held by her one-time vassals in the land they had called Djahi.

In the last years of the Egyptian empire there was a political take-over in Upper Egypt by the High Priest of Amon-Re. The priestly clan of Roma-Roy and, after them, of Ramessesnakht rejoiced in the power and wealth they had and tried to extend them, yet these priestly dynasties turned out not to be long lasting. The High Priesthood at Thebes rarely passed from father to son for more than three generations and then a new family grouping took over. In theory they were always vulnerable to intervention by pharaoh no matter how independent the regime at Thebes might be in fact. But what really prevented a self-perpetuating sacerdotal society in the long run was the very extent of temple possessions and patronage. Even if pharaoh was impotent, the seat of Amon-Re was a prime objective in any period of political instability for ambitious men with power behind them. After the civil war in the south, Herihor, Commander of the Southern Army, seized the office of High Priest for himself. No doubt the image of Amon-Re was brought out in his shrine to make an oracular pronouncement in Herihor's favour, whose power was thereby legitimized. Herihor, that is to say, was not a High Priest who took over Upper Egypt; he was a general who took over the High Priesthood and established a dynasty.

In Lower Egypt the priests of Re-Harakhte at Heliopolis and the priests of Ptah at Memphis had no political pretensions beyond the accumulation of wealth and patronage in the interests of their respective deities. Nesbenebded of Tanis, who had confiscated Wenamon's credentials, was not a priest but a Delta nobleman with a wife who may have had royal blood in her veins and so he found it easy to assume the title and dignities of pharaoh when his nominal lord, Ramesses IX, died in Memphis.

The innate conservatism of the Egyptians saw to it that whether a soldier or a priest was in power they lacked the self-awareness to adapt to a changed world in which new, aggressive powers were stirring. Where there had once been a national interest to consider, there were now individual ambitions; instead of an awareness of the presence of the gods only the forms of observance remained. *Ma'at* was rarely invoked. A belief that man was, in spite of hardship and suffering, at home in the universe was replaced by superstition and in courtly circles a meticulous observance of ritualistic detail as though the new devils of uncertainty could be exorcized by ceremonials. The gods were still great but they were seen to be manipulated by men.

The immense stretches of Egyptian history are such and they happened, by the European scale of things, so long ago that inevitably the rise and fall of dynasties, the triumphs and set-backs, are foreshortened. Wenamon, on his mission to Byblos, knew that Egypt had been trading with that city for over two thousand years. For longer than the time separating us from the celebration of the last morning office of Amon-Re in Roman times, the Egyptians had worshipped Isis and Osiris, the sun-god Re, and the other members of the ancient pantheon. There was a continuity of behaviour and values for which the modern world offers no parallel. The chronicles went back so far that, to the Egyptians, the Egyptian way of life expressed a fundamental truth about existence; the lot of man is unchanging, there is no new thing under the sun. The Egyptian drive to 'extend the frontiers' was a response to the Hyksos shock. When Egyptian dominance in the East came to an end, some sage, a priest in the temple of Ptah, might have argued it was all for the best. Egypt could now be true to itself, its ancient rituals and codes; they would persist whatever pharaoh came, whether he was Egyptian, Nubian, Ethiopian, or whatever.

In this he would be right. Whatever vicissitudes and foreign invasions Egypt was to suffer after the end of the New Kingdom, the Egyptian gods were served in ritual and tribute for more than a thousand years to come. It was Zeus-Amon who confirmed Alexander the Great in his kingship in 331 BC at Siwa and it was with the ram's horns of Amon that he is depicted on his coins. It was Zeus rather than Amon who drew Alexander to Siwa, whose oracle was famous in Greece itself; but the divine king who conquered as far as India and is referred to in the Book of Daniel as 'a rough goat' – ram is really meant – shares with the warrior pharaohs in some vestigial sense a son-ship of 'the Hidden One' by whose name they had once held most of the civilized world in fee.

During the Twentieth Dynasty the tomb robbers had become so active that the royal tombs in the Biban el-Moluk were being stripped of their precious grave furnishings. Gold canopies, mummy cases, jewellery, furniture, weapons were all removed so that in some cases only the mummies of the greatest pharaohs of the previous five hundred years were left. The scandal was so great that Herihor had those of Seti I and Ramesses II removed to a safer place, and later these together with many others were secreted in a small rock tomb at the bottom of a shaft near Deir el-Bahri. They remained there until the 1870s when, once again, tomb robbers, who follow one of the most ancient of Egyptian professions, found them. When in due course the authorities became aware that a lot of surprising objects were coming on to the market, an investigation took place. One of the robbers eventually confessed and the desiccated majesty of the Egyptian empire was found tumbled in disorder.

The royal mummies were brought out, first of all to Luxor and then by Nile steamer to Cairo: Seqenenre with his axe-shattered skull and mouth agape, Amosis conqueror of the Hyksos, Amenophis I, Tuthmosis II, Tuthmosis III with his beaked nose, Seti I looking benign and professional like a Victorian High Court judge, Ramesses I, Ramesses II. Nearly all the great names were there together with thirty others. Maspero, the Cairo Museum director and distinguished Egyptologist, recorded what he subsequently called 'a curious thing'. As the funerary craft moved north, crowds appeared on both banks of the Nile, for more than twenty miles, from Luxor to Kuft. This is no uncommon thing in itself. A steamer is an object of great interest and to this day is cheered from the banks by laughing children who run, or whip up their donkeys, to keep up.

But in July 1881 the demonstration was different. Peasant women wailed in mourning and ran with dishevelled hair, as at a funeral. Their menfolk fired shots in the air, which was another funerary custom. Cynics say they were mourning the loss of a source of income but this cannot be true. The tomb robbers were a small group of specialists who had kept their skills and secrets in the family for generations and they did not spread their gains around. This was a genuine, mourning salute. Egyptian peasants are simple people with an immensely long folk-memory; they also have an innate sense of propriety and would not have conducted themselves as they did if they had not, however dimly, understood they were attending on dead kings who were Egyptian like themselves and had ruled in splendour before the foreigners came.

SOURCE BOOKS

This narrative for the general reader is heavily indebted to the scholarship of Professor J. H. Breasted; Dr A. Erman; Sir Alan Gardiner; Mr J. A. Wilson; Mr Cyril Aldred and the contributors to *The Cambridge Ancient History* particularly Mr T. G. H. James and the late William C. Hayes; and to many others. To keep the story flowing I have avoided footnotes and numbered references but anyone curious to know the authority for some of the more surprising information should have no difficulty in checking it against the books listed below. I am thinking particularly of the suggestion that Tutankhamon did not die a natural death and that the family of Queen Tiy, though she was a commoner, was of greater importance for the Eighteenth Dynasty than had been realized before Mr Aldred gave some of the background. This is still a matter of debate among scholars, as indeed are many other aspects of ancient history. Certainty is elusive. At times I have followed one line rather than another because it seemed to lead to a more coherent picture. But for the most part my account presents the generally agreed findings of recent Egyptology.

Cyril Aldred, *Akhenaten, Pharaoh of Egypt, a New Study* (London, 1968)

Cyril Aldred, *Egypt: the Amarna Period and the end of the 18th Dynasty* (Cambridge, 1971)

O. Bates, *The Eastern Libyans* (London, 1914)

Dr Manfred Bietak, of the Austrian Institute in Cairo, 'Avaris and Per-Ramesse', the Mortimer Wheeler lecture at the British Academy, May 1979 (London, 1979)

A. M. Blackman, 'Oracles in Ancient Egypt', *Journal of Egyptian Archaeology*, vol. 11 (1925) and vol. 12 (1926)

J. H. Breasted, *Ancient Records of Egypt*, vols. II, III, and IV (New York, 1906)

J. H. Breasted, *History of Egypt*, 2nd edition (New York, 1948)

R. A. Caminos, *Late Egyptian Miscellanies* (Oxford, 1954)

J. Cerny, *Ancient Egyptian Religion* (London, 1952)

I. E. S. Edwards, C. J. Gadd, N. G. L. Hammond, and E. Sollberger, eds., *The Cambridge Ancient History*, vol. II, Parts 1 and 2 (Cambridge, 1973 and 1975)

Walter Emery, *Egypt in Nubia* (London, 1965)

A. Erman, *Literature of the Ancient Egyptians*, trans. A. M. Blackman (London, 1927)

Sir Alan Gardiner, *Egypt of the Pharaohs* (Oxford, 1961)

B. Gunn, 'Religion of the Poor in Ancient Egypt', *Journal of Egyptian Archaeology*, vol. 3 (1916)

W. C. Hayes, *The Scepter of Egypt*, Parts 1 and 2 (New York, 1953; Harvard, 1959)

G. Lefebvre, *Histoire des Grandes Prêtres d'Amon de Karnak* (Paris, 1929)

Björn Landström, *Ships of the Pharaohs* (London, 1970)

S. A. B. Mercer, *The Tell el-Amarna Tablets*, 2 vols (Toronto, 1939)

J. B. Pritchard, ed., *Ancient Near East Texts relating to the Old Testament* (Princeton, 1955)

T. Säve-Söderbergh, *The Navy of the 18th Dynasty* (Uppsala, 1946)

A. R. Schulman, *Military Rank, Title and Organisation in the Egyptian New Kingdom* (Berlin, 1964)

A. W. Shorter, *Egyptian Religion in the 18th Dynasty* (London, 1931)

G. Steindorff and K. C. Seele, *When Egypt Ruled the East* (Chicago, 1963)

J. A. Wilson, *The Burden of Egypt* (Chicago, 1951)

Yigael Yadin, *The Art of Warfare in Biblical Lands* (London, 1963)

There is considerable variety in the spelling of Egyptian words. The ancient Egyptians recorded only the consonants so the vowels are uncertain. Except for writing the god's name as Amon, I have followed the spelling used in *The Cambridge Ancient History*. The sun-god Re is usually pronounced Ray by Egyptologists and some might prefer to write the name of the god who presided over the Egyptian imperial effort as Amūn-Ray.

ACKNOWLEDGMENTS

Antonia Benedek: p. 62 (top). British Museum: pp. 11, 43, 59, 96 (top), 112, 146. British Museum/Michael Holford: pp. 9 (bottom), 108 (bottom), 109 (both). Cairo Museum/Hassia: pp. 71, 75, 105, 117, 119, 120, 121, 129, 131, 139, 189. Cairo Museum/Middle East Photographic Archive: p. 22. Peter Clayton: pp. 9 (top), 12–13, 34, 45, 146 (all), 149 (both), 156–7, 191 (bottom). Sonia Halliday: pp. 47, 161. Hassia: pp. 7, 31, 38, 53, 55, 64, 69, 79, 83, 87, 91, 99 (both), 102, 108 (top), 122, 137, 141, 148, 153, 177, 180, 181, 188. Michael Holford: pp. 25 (top), 26, 48 (both), 73, 96 (bottom), 169 (top). William MacQuitty: pp. 107, 155 (bottom), 192. Fred Maroon: pp. 14, 74, 110, 143, 155 (top), 158, 191 (top). Middle East Photographic Archive: pp. 62, 169 (bottom), 170. Ronald Sheridan: pp. 25 (bottom), 60–1, 95, 187, 199, 204.

Maps: A. R. Garrett
Picture Research: Paul Snelgrove

INDEX